On The Beat

On The Beat

With Black Shrimp

Angling Experiences
of a Lifetime

ISBN 978-0-9556267-0-8

Designed and typeset by
Dougie Gibson, Itsallgood Graphic Design,
Cromdale, Grantown-on-Spey, Morayshire.
info@itsallgood.org.uk

Printed and bound by
Biddles Ltd, www.biddles.co.uk

For Anna

The Brae Water of the River Spey, scene of many fine catches

Contents

1

Foreword

Early in the 1970s the Highland News, a weekly newspaper published for the Inverness and Highland area, introduced a fishing column which quickly became required reading for anglers throughout the area and beyond. Apparently it boosted circulation by over 500 copies.

The author of the column was Black Shrimp, the nom-de-plume of self-confessed angling nut John Cathcart with whom very many of us, from all over the country, have fished northern waters. We enjoy his relaxed company, admire his angling prowess and are proud to call him friend. During his tenure of the column, stretching over more than 10 years, John reported on catches of British record brown trout and astounding sport with salmon and sea trout when runs were at their peak. He offered a host of tackle tips and regaled readers with extraordinary experiences on river, loch and sea.

His writings informed and entertained. They left you wanting more and looking forward to next week's report. They encouraged you to pick up your rod and go fishing. Starved of information while John took a break in the close season, it was like going cold turkey until the appearance of the first column of the next season!

Black Shrimp – adopted from the now famous fly John invented in memory of his close friend Steve Fraser after his tragic death at the age of 27 – has now put together a wonderful collection of tales from a lifetime's experiences of fishing in pleasant and productive places, and shooting on some of the Highlands' top estates.

This book reflects John's enduring passion for the sport and his unique understanding of the freshwater environment. It records over half a century of Highland angling history and reminds the elders among us of great days gone by. Hopefully, it will stimulate the interest of the next generation and inspire them to develop the skills and enthusiasm for angling for which Inverness exponents of the noble art are renowned. One thing is certain: once again Black Shrimp is bound to become required reading by anglers far and wide.

Alan Scott

2

Introduction

I was first afflicted with the incurable condition – an interest in fish and fishing – over 65 years ago when I graduated from fishing for tiny brown trout in small Highland streams to casting for salmon in broad bold rivers such as the Tay, Spey and Ness, to name but a few.

During this time I have been lucky enough to have landed several thousand salmon and trout. These experiences have left their marks and, for a long time now, friends have been saying that I should commit them to paper. Now that I have retired and have a lot of time on my hands, I thought, why not? Give it a go.

I hope that readers will enjoy my recollections of many sporting experiences. Perhaps one of these may prompt the odd smile as it recalls personal memories of your own. Tight lines anyway.

3

Acknowledgements

When I first thought seriously about writing my book I soon realised that hand writing the scripts was only the beginning. I had to have them typed and proof-read long before the final manuscript was ready for publication.

That is when my old friend Alan Scott volunteered to assist me. He had just retired after a lifetime's involvement in journalism and press and public relations so typing didn't present any difficulties. Just as important from my point of view Alan has been a serious and successful salmon angler for as long as I have known him, so who better could I have to proof-read my scribblings? I am greatly indebted to him for all his help and advice, without which my book would never have been completed. Thanks pal!

I would also like to thank several other people who helped me greatly by filling in blanks while I was researching items to finish the book – George Cameron, honorary vice president of Inverness Angling Club; Dennis Young; Scott MacKenzie of Ness Side, Inverness; and Mr and Mrs Campbell, parents of the late Malcolm Campbell.

John Cathcart
Black Shrimp

How it all began

My introduction to the noble art

My first recollection of anything to do with fish was in the years before the war – no, not the 1914-18 one! – when I went camping with my father, mother and eldest sister Margaret to the Spittal of Glenshee, between our home in Blairgowrie and Braemar. At the age of five I clearly remember, somewhat bemused, watching my father lying on the bank of a small tumbling stream no more than two to three feet wide and, sleeves rolled up, putting his hands under the overhanging bank. After what seemed no more than a few seconds, father – who, incidentally, never ever held a fishing rod – came out clutching a beautifully marked golden trout. He repeated this several times until we had sufficient to take back to the camp site where mother cleaned and cooked them, in a frying pan, for our supper. They certainly were small but I do remember they were delicious.

No matter how many times I tried guddling or tickling, as this practice is known, I could not master the art. Although I often felt the trout under the bank with my fingertips, I could not catch hold of them. Perhaps my fingers were too short then.

About the same time my uncle Donald, who would have been about 10 years older than me, came camping with us and I used to accompany him when he fished the River Shee which ran past our camp site. His tackle, as I remember, was pretty rudimentary, consisting of a two piece greenheart rod and a basic brass reel. His line was brown cord with a length of gut attached to a small bait hook. Worms were the bait. I can remember that, if we crawled quietly up to the edge of one of the deeper pools and did not expose ourselves, we could see shoals of trout in the gin-clear water. The largest would hardly have been more than a quarter of a pound. Catching them wasn't at all easy and Donald had his best sport when the river was in flood and coloured. This seemed to happen every time we were camping as it always seemed to be raining then. When Donald caught a fish he unhooked it and threw it to me and I would sit on top of the poor creature until it stopped wriggling.

These experiences were repeated for a number of years until my father was called up. But, unquestionably, I had been hooked and to this day I have been unable to diminish the urge to go fishing!

Following my introduction to the noble art, and on my return home, I had to get myself some fishing tackle. But how could I possibly afford to buy a rod and line? A number of local boys of about my age fished the River Ericht near my home. Their outfits comprised a four to five foot long cane or stick with brown cord line wrapped around the end. The well off boys would have real hooks to gut, but I had to make do with a bent pin (honest!) which I tied, heaven knows by what knot, to a piece of gut.

The River Ericht is up to 60 yards wide at Blairgowrie and near my home the bottom was of solid rock, with deep fissures. Trout stayed well out from the bank but in the shallows were shoals of minnows which we called Baggie minnows. They grew to about three inches long at best and had no culinary value. We used to turn over stones in the shallows and gather caddis grubs in their protective jackets made with grains of sand. The baggies loved these grubs and I recall wading in the shallows, bare-footed and thigh deep, until I saw a shoal. Dropping the baited pin among the fish, I watched until it was grabbed by the greediest baggie then yanked it over my head and invariably lost it in the water or on the bank behind me.

During the war years when we could not go camping, mother used to pack me off every summer to the Spittal of Glenshee where I was given accommodation by Millie MacLean and her shepherd brother Jim at 'The Coombes'. Jim fished a bit but he was not inclined to divulge any secrets of the game to a tousle-headed lad frae Blair.

I had by this time managed to acquire an old greenheart fishing rod and brass reel but the same strike and yank over the head method of landing a fish prevailed. The only thing the reel was used for was storing the line when not in use.

The years rolled on and my fishing experiences were restricted to the Ericht, the Shee and several local tributary burns of the Ericht. The largest fish I managed to land, from the Lornty Burn by the usual strike and yank method, weighed six ounces.

My first poacher

I remember a summer in Blairgowrie, when I was about 10 years old, crossing the bridge leading to Rattray and, as always, looking over in case there was a salmon in the pool below. This was a regular event when running salmon were caught there after a quick drop in the water level. Occasionally I saw one there from my bird's eye position.

On the downstream side of the bridge there was a sloping concrete area, a fish pass, which fish used to swim up in big water into a deep pool just below the bridge itself. A few yards upstream of the bridge was a weir which salmon could only pass over if the water was high. Sometimes, fish were trapped between the slope and the weir and very few survived! I suppose there were water bailiffs, but it was wartime and I never saw one.

When I looked over into the pool that day I could see a very large salmon swimming about and a lad in his teens was casting

Me aged five with sister Margaret in Glenshee

at the fish. I cannot now remember what bait or lure he had but I now know that the fish was frightened and kept shooting about the pool in a demented fashion.

I had to get closer to see more. Taking some back streets opposite the Well Meadow, I got down to the river bank at the side of the pool. By this time the fish had disappeared from view and two other big lads had arrived, one in his late teens and the other a bit older than me. I knew them to be brothers from a family who even I had heard of as being poachers.

The older brother had a long, very strong greenheart rod fitted with a massive brass reel holding a thick cord line. Just then another lad of about my age shouted that he had found the fish. By looking carefully into the bridge foundations, I could just see the tail of the salmon sticking out from underneath a large stone.

I stood very close to the brothers as the elder tied on a huge flat double hook which had each hook lying at 180 degrees to each other. From memory, this must have measured at least 2½ inches point to point. I had never seen such a big hook. Indeed, it was bigger than I would use today to fish for cod.

Even at that age I knew a bit about hooks and how to bait them and I watched in amusement as the eldest brother impaled a tiny worm on to the point of one of the hooks. After winding in the line until the hook stopped at the top of the rod, he plunged the rod into the water down towards where I had seen the fish. Seconds later he lifted the point of the rod out of the water and the reel began to scream. He had hooked the fish!

I cannot remember much about the playing of the fish but I do know that it didn't take long before the poor thing was dragged out of the water on to a concrete slab. The big lad handed the rod to his brother and killed the fish with a blow to the head with a baton-like instrument he produced from his pocket. (He must have been a Boy Scout!)

Next – and this is something I will never forget – he pulled the huge hooks out of the fish's flanks, leaving large flaps of skin, opened its mouth and tore the inside of the mouth using the hooks. Even then I understood that this was for the benefit of any bobby or bailiff who might catch them with the fish. They could then say, "Look, we caught it by the mouth sir!" How they could explain away the two tears in its flank, I don't know. "Must have been a seal sir?"

Although it is an awful long time ago, I still think that fish would have been around 20 pounds.

The move to Inverness

My father was demobbed in 1945 and we again went camping to Glenshee for a couple of years. Unfortunately, my father's tailors business, which had been closed over the war years, was proving difficult for him and he was offered a job in a long-established business in Inverness. This meant that the family would have to move north.

By this time I was a regular customer in Blairgowrie's fishing tackle shop, Crockarts in Allan Street. The then owner and friend Harry Michie told me that there was good fishing up in Inverness and that among the fish they caught were sea trout. I had only heard of this fish and, to my knowledge, none were ever caught in the Ericht.

I was an obstinate lad then and I remember putting pressure on my parents saying that I would not move to Inverness unless I got a proper fishing rod! The easiest way for my parents was, I suppose, to give in and I became the proud owner of a two piece nine foot cane rod with a brass reel and cord line. By now nylon was on the market, with French-made probably being the best, and I recall buying it in metre lengths from Harry. This was vastly superior to gut which was still being used for most fly casts. These had to be immersed in a saucer of water the night before going fishing, otherwise knots could not be tied as the gut was too brittle.

When I arrived in Inverness in 1947, the first place I headed for was the river and I just couldn't believe the width of it. At that time there were three constructions crossing the Ness below the castle. The uppermost was known as the temporary bridge, below it was the old suspension bridge and below that was a wooden structure erected to form a new bridge to replace the suspension bridge, the construction of which had been halted after the outbreak of war.

That summer, standing on the temporary bridge and looking upstream into the Castle Pool, all one could see were countless silver flashes as the finnock (small sea trout) rubbed their flanks on the river bed in an attempt to get rid of the sea lice.

I watched every evening as the men with chest waders, including Jack Fraser Snr, Jocky MacDonald, Bob MacIntyre, Charlie MacLennan, William MacKintosh and Mr Campbell – to name only a few – stood in a semi-circle above the bridge and landed fish after fish which, according to size, they either put into their fishing baskets or returned. I immediately became a junior member of Inverness Angling Club. Of course, I did not have waders but shorts and plimsoles sufficed. Obviously, I could not reach the deeper water but I fished the margins with a little success.

By this time I had graduated to fly fishing but had no idea what flies to use. Anglers will appreciate that the choice of flies is endless but I was not shy at asking one of my elders, if I saw he was having a lot of success, "What fly are you using, mister?" I remember one day standing on Ness Walk near the Cathedral watching an elder taking fish after fish from the Black Stream. Naturally, I asked him what fly he was using and he told me it was a Peter Ross. I immediately made my way to Grahams in Union Street where John Hogg, the manager, sold me the first fly I ever bought. The previous ones I used had either been given to me or I had bartered with other youngsters who, like me, were keen on fishing.

Over the years this pattern took a high percentage of all the sea trout and brown trout I landed, and for that I am ever grateful to the late Warden MacIntyre, the then secretary of Inverness Angling Club.

My first big fly rod

My little cane rod wasn't standing up to the extremes I was putting it to and I was on the lookout for a replacement. At that time there were advertisements in newspapers offering three piece, 12 foot steel tank aerials for 7/6d. My pocket money just about covered that and I duly sent for one. It had screw joints and was, even in comparison to greenheart, very heavy. But it looked the part.

About the same time I met another young angler on the river bank and he had a large, four inch salmon reel with an odd drum which was concave in shape. It also had a part missing, as a broken stub beside the reel seat indicated. I did a deal with the lad, 'Kansas' MacKenzie, for half a crown (2/6d or 12½ pence today) and three trout flies. What I didn't know was that I had bought my first spinning reel. The name Mallochs of Perth on it meant nothing to me then, but I reckoned it would make an ideal fly reel for my new 12 footer.

I did not have any cork or knowledge of how to make a handle, but I had plenty string! I made up the handle with layers of string, each one painted with some old paint that was in our garden shed, until I reached the desired thickness. I then bound the reel on with more string before painting the whole handle to give it a nice finish. The rod rings were bound on with insulating tape and the rod was ready for use. To complete the kit, I needed a fly line and one of the elders on the river gave me a bit of an old silk line, no more than 20 yards long. String, of course, served as backing.

It was now the spring of 1948 and fly fishing for trout and wading bare legged were a bit impracticable, so I spent my spare time going down to the river and watching the elders fishing. Practically all of them were spinning and I realised then that my Malloch was in fact a spinning reel. All that was missing from mine was the large loop (coil breaker) which should have been where the broken stub was. A piece of fence wire bent into a loop, with the join covered in sticky tape to smooth it off, was slid underneath the reel seat and bound firmly in place with more string to complete the job. I realised that the three piece 12 foot rod was not suitable for spinning so I made a short insert with a porcelain point ring which I stuck into the top of the eight foot length and this was my spinning rod. I was ready to start spinning.

My first salmon

At this time I was working as a 'boucher' (message boy) for

William Low in the High Street. My meagre wages were supplemented by tips and, at last, I had some money in my pocket.

In April of 1948 the talk on the river was that Jack Stirling, a club member, had caught a seven pound brown trout in the Red Braes Pool. I had no idea at all where the Red Braes Pool was. Passing the Castle Pool a day or so later, I saw a regular fisher of that pool, Dan 'The Bank' Grant, and asked him where the pool was. Armed with the information, I decided to pay the location a visit. First, I had to get some spinning tackle. As I had my tips in my pocket, I went into Woolworths – which at that time sold fishing tackle under the trade name 'Catch em Alive-O' – and purchased a 1½ inch silver devon minnow. My next stop was Grahams where John Hogg sold me a 100 metre spool of five pound Bell nylon. This was the heaviest line I could buy with what was left of my tip money.

When I got home I put some blue paint on the back of the lure, because that was the colour of the lures I had seen the men on the river using, and pushed some slivers of lead inside to make it heavier so that it would cast further.

The next day I arranged with two of my pals, Willie Nairn and Brian Matheson, to accompany me on my expedition. The Red Braes Pool was not terribly far from where I stayed in Ballifeary Road and on our arrival at the bottom of the pool – above the weir upstream of Holm Mills – I commenced fishing up the pool, being totally ignorant of the fact that the proper way to fish was from the top down. I suppose I must have fished for about an hour and moved some 200 yards upstream when, as the lure was being retrieved, it stopped and then tugged! Naturally, I thought I had hooked a big brown trout and began to play it. Never before had I hooked a fish which actually took line off the reel but, boy, this one did!

I now realise that my ignorance of how to play a fish, and

particularly that I made no attempt to put extra tension on the fish as it ran, saved the day. Otherwise, the five pound breaking strain line would not have survived the extra pressure. The fact that the line was brand new and completely unstrained was also a major factor in my eventual success.

I was still convinced that I was playing a trout but suddenly, during one of its many long runs, I saw this huge silver fish jump at the end of my line and realised it was a salmon.

Standing on the weir opposite me was George Cameron Snr who was the then groundsman at Bellfield Park. He began shouting advice on how to play it. It was playing me! I did not have a net or gaff so I shouted to George, "How do I land it?" He replied, "Tail it." I responded, "What does that mean?" as I had never heard that expression before. He explained that you first put a handkerchief on your hand then gripped the fish around the tail and lifted it out of the water.

The fish must have been on for perhaps an hour by then and was gradually coming nearer and nearer the bank. Willie wet his hanky, put it over his hands and as the fish swam close to him, bent and grabbed the fish by the tail with both hands and lifted it from the water. Half way up the bank he lost his grip and dropped the fish which slithered straight between his legs out into the middle of the river. Willie calmly grabbed hold of the line and stepped over it. Poor George must have been having kittens watching this fiasco but I can't remember what he shouted.

The fish soon came into range again. To his eternal credit, Willie removed his ex-Army battle blouse top and, when the fish got close to the bank, he slipped the jacket under it, fell on top of it and started punching it with his fists! Meantime, Brian had gathered a pile of stones and a stick which he offered to Willie saying, "Kill it, kill it!"

The fish was duly dispatched and unhooked, the small size 12 treble being right in the corner of its mouth, and placed higher up the bank. George was alternately mopping his brow and clapping his hands!

I cannot explain what I felt then, but I just had to have another cast – without retying all the knots as I now advocate. But I was only a laddie then and didn't know about things like that. Would you believe it? I hooked another one! This one, however, did not stay hooked for long and we decided it was time to go home.

My first salmon weighed 22½ pounds and it took me many, many years before I bettered that one. I often think that had I not landed such a large salmon for my first fish, would I have continued to be as keen as I am today?

I took up spinning quite seriously after that and 10 to 12 pound nylon spinning line replaced the string backing for my fly line. The fly line was coiled up in an envelope and kept in my bag to be tied on to the end of the spinning line when fly fishing was to be the order of the day.

My first salmon on the fly

Later in the summer of that same year, I was watching the old brigade fishing in the Castle Pool and one of them, Jack Fraser Snr, was having a great time landing many trout. When he waded ashore, I asked him, "What fly were you using, sir?" He told me that it was a Blue Charm, a salmon fly previously unheard of by me. I went up to Grahams the next morning where I asked John Hogg if I could have a Blue Charm. He asked me what I wanted it for and I told him that I had seen a man catching sea trout with one the previous evening. He then asked if I could afford to buy one as they cost 7/6d each, then a small fortune for one fly. As I had just about that amount I agreed to buy one. He gave me a size eight double and it wasn't long before I had tied it to the end of a length of 10 pound nylon attached to the end of my silk line

I went to the Black Stream, where I had previously seen Warden MacIntyre fishing. Using the 12 foot aerial fly rod, I hooked a fish – which I soon realised was a salmon – on my first run down the pool. It was during the tourist season and I soon had a gallery all shouting advice such as "Let it go" and "Bring it in now laddie". I quickly learned that no matter how well intentioned the advice, it was up to me to do what I thought was right. The fish, a beautiful clean run eight pounder, was duly landed by a helpful spectator.

One thing I remember clearly about this incident was panicking every time the knot between the 10/12 pound nylon spinning line and the 20 yard long fly line ran off the reel. I wasn't happy until the knot was safely back on the reel.

The Malloch reel and steel aerial rod remained faithful servants to me for a number of years, although the number of salmon I caught was not too great. But I continued to land a reasonable number of sea trout annually, mostly on the fly.

My first proper job

Almost before I knew it, I had turned 16 and left school. What was I going to do? I had no particular interest in taking up a trade such as a joiner or electrician. But mother insisted that I start working and arranged for me to start as an apprentice coachbuilder with Jock MacLeod at his premises in King Street.

I must admit I hated it and, within a few weeks, I gave him my notice. I had made enquiries at Grahams to see if they had any vacancies for an apprentice and, after an interview with Grahams' then owner, Col Bruce-Watt, I began work there. I was assigned to the back shop to work under George Masson repairing tennis and badminton rackets, and fishing rods. I learned how to whip on rings, replace ferrules and cork handles, clean and oil guns and rifles, and various things connected with general sporting life.

I recall that we were extremely busy just prior to August 12, cleaning and oiling shotguns which had been stored in the shop by their owners since they had last used them at the end of the previous grouse season. Another task undertaken on the premises was the loading of shotgun cartridges, mainly 12 bore. Safety while working with gunpowder was extremely well maintained.

My boss was, of course, John Hogg, a tall red-headed man who always wore tweed suits of the plus four style. He had an odd sense of humour and I was often the butt of his jokes. On one occasion I was sent round to the nearby ironmongers, Gilbert Ross, to buy a tin of 'sky blue scarlet paint'. On another occasion he handed me a shotgun which he told me to 'clean outside'. Naturally, I thought that he meant me to clean the outside of the gun and began to do just that. John then came back and asked me if I had understood what he had said, and repeated his instructions. I felt a right fool standing on the pavement outside the shop cleaning the gun, but in those days you did what you were told.

Working in the front shop at that time was Bill Brown who became one of the most respected figures in the shooting/fishing scene in the Highlands and a very good friend.

In the early 1950s fixed spool reels began to appear on the market. These included the Hardy Altex, the Ambidex, Felton Crosswind and the working man's reel, the Mitchell 300. I bought a Mitchell and the difference in the distance we could cast compared with the Malloch – and the lack of bird's nests of tangled lines which were a daily experience with the Malloch – became things of the past. I remember that almost half the time on the river was spent sitting on the bank untangling lines.

In those days ball bearing swivels, now an everyday part of a spinner's rig, were unheard of and the efficiency of the barrel swivels we then used was poor at best. Added to that was the fact that the Malloch reel mechanics involved turning the reel sideways to cast, thereby putting twists on the line. The reel drum was turned back to a forward facing position before the line was rewound on to the spool, with the twists still present.

After a number of casts twists built up on the line until it was so badly twisted that it would jump off the reel into a bird's nest. The best way to remove the twists was to hook the line on to a bush, walk out the length of a cast, lay down the rod and cut off the lure. The exposed line was then taken for a walk through bushes or long grass until the twists had all been forced off the line. The line was then rewound, the lure retied to the end of the line and off we could go again. This procedure would be repeated many times during a day's fishing but it was quicker than trying to undo tangles by hand.

Tangles can still happen with fixed spool reels which put twists on the line while casting but these are negated by the pick-up when the line is rewound on to the spool. The problem of excessive twists occurs mostly as a result of a fouled swivel and the method I've explained is still the most efficient way to straighten out the line.

I also bought a 13 foot split cane fly rod with a matching reel and a double tapered Kingfisher silk fly line. I was then pretty well up to date as far as tackle was concerned.

I was settling into a nice relaxed rhythm with my life – no girlfriends and plenty of time to fish. Alas, all good things come to an end and in 1952 I was called up to do my National Service. I chose the RAF and, because they paid more money for the extra year over the compulsory two years, I signed on for three years. What a twit I was!

My three years in the RAF

Friends and football

I was due to leave Inverness by train in the early afternoon of July 1, 1952, but that gave me time to go fishing first. I started at the Legion Pool and was delighted to catch one of the first grilse of the season, weighing five pounds. I then cycled up to the MacIntyre Pool where I landed a magnificent 20 pounder. These were the last salmon I was to catch for over three years.

My first posting, after square bashing and trade training as a nursing attendant in Lytham St Annes, was to Yatesbury in Wiltshire. Despite a good look round, I never saw any angling going on in the area. But I was quite keen on football, having played for Muirpark (Caledonian FC Juvenile) and Clach Rangers under 18s, then managed by the late ex-Chelsea player George Rodgers. I asked around locally and found that Calne and Harris United, playing in the Wiltshire league, were looking for a goalkeeper. I had a trial game and signed up with them. Getting Saturdays off wasn't always easy, so I did not play an awful lot of games for them. I was working as a nursing attendant in the camp's sick quarters and had by now been promoted to the elevated rank of Leading Aircraftsman (LAC).

After about 18 months there I was posted to Germany and ended up as the only medic in a new RAF hospital at Wegberg, situated in open country near Cologne and Dusseldorf. Among the staff there were a couple of RAF policemen, a couple of cooks, a driver and about eight or 10 admin orderlies. Our CO was an admin Sergeant. Also on the camp were some German civilians, male and female, and I was put in charge of a number of the tasked with jobs as diverse as collecting loads of coal from a nearby railway station to cleaning wards and corridors after the builders had finished working there.

I made friends with one of these Germans, a Willy Kutski, who lived just outside the camp near the small village of Broich Peel, where I spent a lot of my off-duty time with Willy and his wife Anna. His parents lived nearby in what I would call a smallholding. They had a few fields, some cultivated and others as grazing for a few animals. I shall never forget being invited to the smallholding one evening. The occasion was the killing of one of their pigs, and everything we ate and drank that night was dedicated to the poor old sow. Sausages of various description were made using the blood and intestines and who knows what else. Other parts of the animal were salted and smoked for putting away to feed the family over the forthcoming winter months.

Broich Peel, I soon learned, had a football team and enquiries resulted in my being signed on. Their pitch, as with every other pitch I saw and played on, was made of cinders and playing bare kneed resulted in some very nasty dirty grazes. I soon acquired a pair of 'knee-shoen' (elasticated knee pads), a pair of padded shorts and a pair of padded gloves. These certainly prevented me getting too many injuries.

Fishing in Germany

Outside the front gates of the camp was the small lake Bush Mulle, with a pub on its banks. About half a mile further down the road was a similar sized lake known as Holtz Mulle. I passed these lakes every time I was going to the village of Wegberg but, despite looking carefully each time I passed, I never saw any sign of fish life.

One day, however, as I was passing Bush Mulle, I saw a man with a fishing rod and reel. The rod was of glass fibre, only the second one I had seen (the first being an American one when I worked a Grahams), and a reel of an unknown fixed spool type. I had no

German then, although I later spoke a little of the language, but I began a 'conversation' which, to a bystander, must have been quite hilarious to watch and listen to. The outcome was that he sold me the outfit for the equivalent of £9 in D/Marks. I did not have cash to the value and arranged to meet him at the same place the following week.

Returning to the camp, I wrote home to my mother asking her to forward me the cash. On its arrival a few days later I converted it into D/Marks and returned to Bush Mulle at the appointed time. I was pleasantly surprised when Heinz, as I knew him, turned up with the rod and reel and, very importantly, a selection of spoon lures. The deal was done. I began to spend every off-duty moment on both lakes and landed quite a number of pike, up to six to eight pounds, and small perch.

None of the lads on the camp expressed any interest in eating these fish. Nevertheless, I banged them on the head, as I had always done at home where I considered these fish to be vermin, and left them lying on the banks. They were picked up by locals who I assume took them home to eat.

My most frightening moment ever

My fishing activities on German lakes resulted in one of the most frightening experiences of my life. I left the camp after work as usual one evening to fish the lakes and this time, purely by chance, two of my billet mates, Chris Wright and Tom Jones, decided to accompany me. I was fishing Holtz Mulle after having landed and killed two small pike when two burly Germans dressed in green uniform with Tyrolean hats and shotguns across their shoulders came up. They began speaking to me, obviously in German, and I could understand enough to know that they were telling me that I should not be fishing there. I pled ignorance and kept replying, "Nix furtein" (I don't understand) This went on for a few minutes and then, without warning, larger of the two Germans – who I gathered were game wardens – snatched the rod from my grasp and handed it to his colleague. I was frightened, to say the least, but this rod and reel had cost me £9 and I was determined to try to get it back.

Stepping towards the big German, I told him in my best German that this was 'verboten' and he could not do this. He stepped forward and gave me a push in the chest. I was a skinny wee lad in those days, weighing no more than 10½ stone, and the result was that I was sent flying on to my back. But I quickly jumped back to my feet and faced up to him, my heart racing and my knees buckling. He stepped back and I thought for a minute that he was going for his shotgun. But then he put his hand inside his waistcoat. I fully expected him to produce a hand gun, but what he drew out and pointed at me – just a few inches from my chest – was a huge knife. I can honestly say I have never been so scared in my life and the only thing I could think of was pulling out my sheath knife which was hidden from view under my jacket. I pointed it at his chest and I know that if he had made any further move towards me I would have used it!

Clearly, everyone was in shock at the way this incident had deteriorated. I can still remember my German's face showing disbelief that this insignificant Schotlander had the nerve to stand up to him. How dare he! There was a pregnant pause when everyone stood motionless. Suddenly, outside my field of vision, my pal Chris Wright grabbed the fishing rod from the second German and yelled, "John, I've got your rod!" The three of us ran off like scalded cats towards the camp and I fully expected to feel the sting of buckshot on my back. Fortunately, this did not happen. I didn't look back and never saw those Germans again.

On our return to camp we went straight to the guardhouse and reported the incident. I heard no more about it but I never went fishing again in Germany, nor would I leave the camp alone.

was demobbed in July 1955 and returned home with my German and reel which saw long and successful service on the Ness.

Night Fishing

Trout on the Laggan

In my honest opinion, there is no more exciting branch of fresh water angling than night fishing for trout, and I regret leaving it so late in my life before I took it up seriously. I realise that, for the best part of my life since moving up to Inverness as a boy, I missed out on this most exhilarating aspect of the noble art.

It is not that I didn't have the opportunity, for in the early days there was an abundance of sea trout in the Ness. I really supposed, however, that one finished at the fall of darkness. Oh boy, what a mistake I made and what great sport I lost!

After completing my National Service and joining the Inverness Burgh Police, I met the late Louis Davidson who then rented the Laggan Pool on the Ness and, a few years later, the Dochfour Fishings, also on the Ness. Louis very kindly invited me to fish both these beats, mainly in the spring when I did land the odd fish, mostly on the spinner.

It was about this time that I met Jack Redpath, a prison officer whose father was the owner of a fishing tackle shop, Watsons in Inglis Street, Inverness. He was the inventor of the Hairy Mary salmon fly, a long time favourite on the Ness and many other Scottish rivers. Its uniqueness was that it was one of the first hair wing flies ever commercially tied.

Jack, a very keen angler, told me that he had his best sport fly fishing for trout after dark and that the Laggan Pool was one of his favourite spots. In July, round about 1960, I went up to the

Laggan Pool just before dark. The river was on the low side and very few salmon had been taken on the Inverness Angling Club waters up to that point in the season. I made up my cast with two flies, a Black Pennel on the bob and a size eight Olive Quill on the tail. When I started fishing at the top of the pool there was a hatch of natural flies and a few trout were rising to these. But the gulls were making the most of this bonanza and I recall that the air was thick with them.

I soon hooked and landed a couple of half pound brownies which were returned, and it was a good hour later before I got my next take. This one took quite a long time to land, when it turned out to be a beautiful brownie of three pounds. I fished until three am, when the fish had gone off completely and the first signs of daylight were beginning to filter through the trees. I had landed 10 brown trout and lost as many, almost all of those landed taking the Olive Quill. I had two at three pounds and the remaining fish weighed in excess of a pound each.

I had a few more nights there over the next few years, with varying degrees of success. Then it was let out to other parties with whom I had no contact, and that was that.

Salmon on the Woolly Bear

The first experience I remember of night fishing on the Spey was at Knockando where I had fished several times courtesy of the late Bob Anderson, the keeper there who I first met while working in Grahams.

During my days there I caught several salmon spinning, but this particular day – it would have been in the late 1950s – I fished on into the dark to see if I could catch a sea trout which I had been told were plentiful then. I do remember that, as a top dropper, I had tied on this large tandem-hooked fly, not dissimilar to a Loch Ordie, which I think was called a Woolly Bear. I got it from the late Willie MacBean and I have never seen one like it since. I do remember that it created quite a wake as it fished round. I picked up a couple of sea trout of about two pounds each on it and continued fishing until two am when I thought, as nothing was happening, I had better call it a night and drive home to Inverness.

I decided to have three more casts and, on the third, cast across the narrow neck of the pool. In the half light, I saw a big swirl at the fly. I waited for a pull but there was nothing. I then saw another two big swirls at the fly and, on the third, the line tightened. I knew as I began to play it that it was a heavy fish and it took some time before I could lead it up into a little backwater where I tailed it. I reckoned my net was too small for the size of fish it was — a beautiful clean run 11 pound salmon which had taken the Woolly Bear.

I was well satisfied with my night's work. As I drove home I pondered that this was the first salmon I had hooked fishing at night. I had been told that salmon did not take at night but I was to prove that wrong a few more times over the years. I never tried fishing floating-type flies again at night. I now wish I had and it was only when writing this story that this was brought back to mind.

Nights on the Ewe

There are other rivers in the Highlands which fish well at night. The next one I fished was the Ewe, which runs out of Loch Maree. The first night I fished it I was accompanied by Willie Armstrong, the present owner of Grahams Tackle Shop in Castle Street, Inverness. I had a really fantastic night, landing 15 sea trout to 3½ pounds and two grilse.

I was fishing a single handed rod, as I always did when night fishing then. The unexpected outcome of that great night was tennis elbow. Believe me, this is a very painful condition which I didn't manage to get rid of until many years later.

That memorable night was the first of many I had on this river. It was the decline of the sea trout stocks in recent years in this, and all other west coast rivers, that ended my trips there. Indeed, it became so bad that any sea trout landed had to be returned.

The rock and the Coachman

There are special things you will always remember about fishing experiences. One such experience happened when I was fishing alone on the River Ewe around 1984. I can't be totally accurate as I have never kept a diary, an omission I will always regret. The sea trout were still relatively plentiful then. I had fished from the onset of darkness, about 11 pm, until some time after midnight without a single offer.

I was fishing two flies on a short stout cast, probably a Black Shrimp on the tail and a Silver Stoat on the dropper. I invariably fished with salmon flies like that as it was not unusual to catch a salmon in the early part of the night, before darkness had fallen. Deciding to change the flies, I knelt down on the bank, opened my fly box, laid it on the ground and placed my torch alongside to illuminate the choice of flies.

As I was pondering over the selection, a moth flew between my eyes and the flies. It was out of focus, but what did make an impression on me was that the blurred insect appeared to be white. By pure chance, early the previous evening, I had been selecting flies to take with me. Spotting an old American-tied size six Coachman in one of my tackle boxes, I had put it into my fly box. I had not used that pattern at night before but, because of the whiteness of the moth, I decided to give it a try and tied it on the dropper. I cannot now recall my choice of tail fly.

I went back to the head of the pool and hadn't been fishing there very long when I got the totally unmistakeable smashing take of a good sea trout and duly landed a beautiful three pound, clean run fish. The fly it had taken was the Coachman which was quickly responsible for another two beauties from the same pool.

I then walked upstream to the Middle Narrows Pool. Within a few minutes of beginning to cast over the neck of the pool, just below the groyne, I saw in the half light a massive swirl just where I imagined the flies would be. There was a heavy pull and I was in again. This was a big one!

I played it for about 10 to 15 minutes with the fish taking several long runs, then obligingly coming back towards me. Then, after bringing the fish in quite close to the bank, everything went absolutely solid. I tried pulling it as tight as possible from well upstream and downstream of where I had been playing it, but no matter what I did the fish remained fixed solid to some underwater obstacle – a large rock, I imagined. As I could still feel the fish pulsing on the taut line, I thought that the tail hook must be snagged. I tried letting the line go slack, hoping that the fish might unsnag itself, but when I wound in the line it was still stuck fast.

This pool is very deep and there was absolutely no question of trying to wade out to try to disengage the line. Such an action would have been extremely dangerous, if not suicidal.

I spent perhaps 20 minutes trying this and that, all to no avail, and realised that I couldn't stay there all night. After all, I was wasting good fishing time! I came up with the idea of trying to make the fish bolt from its anchorage. I thought that if I could throw a large stone close to where the fish was lying, I might be able to frighten it, make the fish move and free the line.

With the aid of my torch I searched the river bank until I found what I thought would be the ideal tool. It was a flatish round stone about two inches thick, the size of a dinner plate and weighing about three pounds. I thought that if I could throw the stone so that it landed flat on the water above the fish, this should make the loudest contact with the water's surface and, hopefully, would have the best chance of frightening the fish.

Holding my rod upright in my left hand, with the reel unchecked and the stone in the palm of my right hand, I made several swings of my arm and threw the stone high into the air aimed at the spot above where I believed the fish to be lying. The stone hit the water with what I would call an almighty splash. Almost immediately the rod was nearly torn from my grasp and the reel began to scream as the line was pulled off it.

I was very pleased, and not a little surprised, to find that my fish was still on and I was beginning to think that I might be into a sea trout of record proportions. Indeed, this was apparently confirmed when I shone my torch into the water and illuminated the fish as it came close to the bank. When I saw the size of the fish, I realised that my net was totally inadequate. I estimated the fish at 12 to 15 pounds, and began to look for a part of the river bank which would be suitable for beaching it on.

The fish made several more runs but eventually became so exhausted that I was able to manoeuvre it between where I was standing and the water's edge. I grabbed it by the tail and carried it up to safety well away from the water. My excitement at landing this fish was somewhat diminished when I realised that it was not a sea trout, as I had hoped, but a salmon of 17 pounds – hooked on the Coachman.

Examining the cast, I found that the blood knot to the dropper had parted from the rest of the cast and the tail fly was gone. My salvation and the fish's fate had been sealed because, in making up the cast using blood knots – as is my custom – I had used the uppermost part of the cast through the blood knot to form the dropper. When the cast had broken at the knot the fly was still left attached.

No more fish were hooked for the remaining part of that night but it goes down as one of my most successful and enjoyable night's fishing ever.

A fish on every cast

On another visit to the Ewe for a night's fishing, I called as usual at the house of the keeper, the late Ken Anderson, before beginning my efforts. He informed me that I should have a good night's sport as the previous night the rods had caught around 20 sea trout of up to seven pounds in weight. I just couldn't wait to put up my rods and begin. I always put up two rods for night fishing, one with a floating line and the other with a sinking line, and both with casts and flies attached to them. It was so much easier to just change a rod in the dark than to change over the lines and tie on casts and flies.

After darkness had fallen, and I had fished McCordies Pool without success, I moved upstream to the Lower Narrows Pool. Then began one of the most wonderful night's sport I have ever experienced. It was almost a fish every cast for the next two hours. The average weight of these sea trout was well over three pounds. I didn't keep count but reckon conservatively that I must have landed in excess of 20 fish. They all fought like tigers and were bars of silver.

There was only one thing wrong with them, however – they were kelts! It was July and I surmised that, because of low water, these fish must have been land-locked further up the system, possibly in Lochs Clair or Coulin, and had only managed to make their way downstream slowly, feeding as they went, to where I encountered them. They were literally only half a mile from the sea but obviously hadn't been in a hurry to go there.

I have no doubt that the previous night's rods had never encountered kelts before and these were what they had also caught. I'll bet they were disappointed when they prepared them for the table. A good lashing of cochineal would have made them look pink-fleshed at least, but I doubt if this would have improved their taste!

The Inverness Professor

The River Spey is renowned as one of the finest salmon and sea trout rivers in Scotland, if not the land. Over the years, I have been lucky enough to have fished many of the finest salmon beats on this river, but I did not have the opportunity to fish for sea trout – the reason being that we finished fishing at around five pm, long before the sea trout fishing began at the onset of darkness.

It was only after 1985, when I had retired from the police and was working for local solicitors, that I had occasion to call at the Dorvack and Revack Estate office near Grantown-on-Spey. When I asked if they had any fishing on the Spey, they confirmed they had a stretch of the river upstream from Boat of Garten, the Kincardine Beat. The estate was owned by Lady Pauline Grant and her husband Dave Nicolson was actually fishing there that afternoon.

After finishing my work at the estate office, I made my way down to the beat where I met up with Dave and his ghillie, the late Norman Stone. After a good blether with them Dave invited me to fish there that week. It was early July and the salmon were very scarce but Norman assured me there was a good head of sea trout in the river. Obviously, the best time to fish for them was after dark.

I fished that night with modest success and then negotiated the lease of the water from the estate office from 11 pm until eight am daily for the next week or so. A syndicate formed with some friends fished the following nights and had some very good catches. Each night we fished we learned a bit more about the water and our catches improved.

I had never considered the Spey above Grantown as being worth fishing. That may very well be the case for salmon but, believe me, in those days that certainly was not the case for sea trout.

About the same time I learned that Kinchurdy, the beat on the opposite side of the river, was available. As this beat had more fishable pools and the rent was not too exorbitant, myself, Bryan Allely, Alec and Charlie MacDonald, and Hugh MacMillan formed a syndicate and took a lease.

We used to have the beat for one week in early July. Our lease was for 24 hours a day, but we were only interested in the night fishing. The cost then was about £30 per person per day – a lot of money, even in those days! I think the first year I fished there I caught 25 fish for the week and on my best night landed seven fish with the best scaling 7½ pounds.

I had a new favourite sea trout fly by then. I started off fishing Norman Stone's Silver Stoat but one evening, before I went up to fish, I was mucking about at the fly tying vice when I recalled a fly I had been given many years earlier, when I was just a boy and which I was told was an excellent sea trout pattern. Although I had lost the original fly, I remembered the dressing which was:

Hook size	*12 to 6 double*
Tail	*Bronze mallard*
Body	*Yellow floss ribbed with black thread*
Hackle	*Red game cock*
Wing	*Bronze mallard*

I had been told by Charlie 'The Plumber' MacLennan, who had given me the fly, that it was called the Professor, but it differed considerably from the fly of that name which could be bought from tackle shops. I called Charlie's dressing the Inverness Professor.

I used the Inverness Professor exclusively during my nights on Kinchurdy and every sea trout I landed was, not unsurprisingly, taken on that fly. But as I was catching more than most of my colleagues, I was happy to keep using it.

Unfortunately, the news of our success leaked out and the rents went up over the next couple of years until they reached £90 per rod per day/night. That was when I and the other members of the syndicate decided enough was enough and we very reluctantly did not renew our lease. After all, we would have been paying that for four hours out of the 24, at best. In my opinion, as that particular beat was not a great salmon prospect at that time of year, it couldn't justify such an expensive outlay.

Two at a time

My last story about night fishing took place around 1986/87 when an old friend, John Hashim, who I had met several years earlier through the late Mrs Boyd, invited me to fish Dochfour which he and his sons had leased.

The river was very low and salmon were not very plentiful. I asked if I could fish at night for trout, thinking that this might offer a better chance of sport. John agreed and told me to take a friend with me. I invited my old buddy Gordon Smith and we got up to the top beat of Dochfour at about 11 pm.

I had devised a new technique for night fishing by then. I had absolute faith in the Inverness Professor and the only thing in doubt was what size I should fish. To answer this quandary I fished three – a size 12 on the top dropper, a size 8 on the middle and a size 6 on the tail. My cast was deliberately very short and of 15 pounds breaking strain nylon. I found that this did not get tangled readily and was easily disentangled should it become so. Besides, the fish were not gut shy in the dark!

Gordon and I went up to the weir and I began fishing the Glory

Hole, a deep hole on the downside of the main flow of water which comes over the weir from Loch Dochfour. Gordon began fishing about 50 yards downstream.

I was casting into the edge of the fast current and letting my flies swing round into the calmer bit of water on the downstream side of the fast water. I repeated this cast a few times then got a very fierce tug and, in the dark, just made out a silvery flash where the flies would have been. I was on! The fish kept going into the fast water and I had great difficulty in keeping in touch with it.

When using the three fly technique in the dark, I preferred not to use a net, for obvious reasons. If possible, I always beached my fish. There was a convenient gravel bar downstream of where I was standing on the weir and I made my way down to that in preparation for beaching the fish.

But something wasn't quite right. The fish was certainly pulling strongly but it just didn't feel normal. I couldn't work out what was amiss. The silver fish, which I could just see breaking the surface, seemed to be going upstream yet the rest of the cast appeared, from the pull on the rod, to be going downstream. I suddenly realised I was into two fish! Eventually, I managed to get both fish into the shallow water where I picked both up by the back of their heads, hooks still attached, and carried them down to Gordon to show him. The fish on the tail fly was a six pound grilse and the one on the top fly was a two pound brown trout. Another example that salmon do take in the dark!

The three fly technique worked well for me when I went night fishing over the next few years. The small flies did well in the early part of the night and, once it was really dark, the larger flies came into their own. Incidentally, the grilse I caught on the Inverness Professor was not the only one I took on that fly in twilight conditions. I have repeated that several times since.

7

My sherry fish

Shortly after I joined the police in 1955, I met a really fine gentleman, Renzo Serafini, who ran a café/restaurant in Academy Street, Inverness, where my senior colleagues introduced me to him. Many a cup of coffee I had in his back shop when I was on the beat.

Renzo fished a little although his main passion was shooting. Through his business connections he met many gamekeepers who, on their visits to Inverness, would call at his premises for refreshments or to collect parcels which he arranged to be left with him. In return, he would be invited to fish or shoot on their estates.

I recall, in the late 1950s when I was enjoying a cup of coffee in his shop, he told me that he had been invited to fish on Loch Stack but, as he wasn't particularly interested in boat fishing, he asked if I would like to go and take Bill Brown from Grahams with me. I jumped at it. To be honest, I had never heard of Loch Stack. Bill showed me where it was and brought out a book which gave details of average catches over the preceding number of years. It was one of the finest sea trout fisheries in Scotland, on a par with Loch Maree.

Having acquired a car by then, I picked up Bill on the appointed date and we headed north. I had been told that there was to be a third member on the trip and I had to pick him up in Beauly. There, for the first time, I met Jock Gibson who was then the keeper at Benula, near Cannich. Through this meeting I enjoyed many days hind stalking on this estate.

The journey to Loch Stack in north-west Sutherland was, on the roads then, quite an expedition but the trip passed in no time with all the stories going around. We duly arrived at the loch where we were allocated a ghillie (unfortunately, I cannot remember his name). He led us down to the jetty where we all climbed on board a big rowing boat. I had never fished from a boat before and the rod I had was a 13 ft cane rod with a silk line – far too long for boat fishing but the only one I had then! We drew lots and agreed to fish in rotation. I drew the stick so that I fished the first full hour then had a half hour break.

I made up a cast of a Badger on the bob, a Grouse and Claret in the middle and a tiny Hairy Mary tube fly on the tail. We rowed out from the jetty and began fishing within a few minutes. I soon had a rise. Being unaccustomed to this type of fishing, I struck and, of course, missed the fish, probably pulling the fly away from it. I had several more huge swirls at my fly but, my fault I guess, I didn't make contact with any of them.

Our ghillie then rowed us into the open loch and we began a drift. I hooked a fish shortly after, perhaps because I could not see the fly, or the fish coming to the fly, because of the waves. Where we had begun to fish the water had been almost flat calm.

This fish took off like nothing I had previously experienced and at about 60 to 70 yards from the boat it jumped. "It's a salmon," I shouted in great excitement but the ghillie said, "Na laddie, it's a sherry fish." I had never heard of that species before and I looked at Bill enquiringly. He just shrugged his shoulders, not knowing either.

The fish made a couple more long runs before I brought it to the side of the boat where the ghillie expertly netted it. Looking at it lying on the deck, I saw it was a sea trout, albeit a big one. I said to the ghillie, "It's a sea trout!" He said, "No, I think it's a sherry fish" then stuck the spring balance hook into its gills, held it up to weigh it and said, "9¾ pounds, it is a sherry fish." It had taken the Hairy Mary tube fly.

He then explained to us, for neither Bill, Jock nor I knew what he was talking about, that the sherry company Williams and Humbert ran a competition for any angler catching a brown trout of four pounds, a sea trout of eight pounds or a salmon of 25 pounds. Successful anglers would be entitled to claim a bottle of sherry as a prize, together with a certificate.

Several more large sea trout, but not as big as my sherry fish, were caught that day which, again, was one of those days I will never forget. Incidentally, over the next few years – in addition to my sea trout prize – I claimed both the brown trout and salmon sherry fish prizes. Another of my regrets is that I didn't keep the certificates. The sherry didn't last long either!

The right connections

In my lifetime I have landed in excess of three thousand salmon from rivers and lochs as far apart as the Tay in the south, the Dionard in the north, the Shiel at Dornie and the Lochy in the west, the Spey, Dee and North Esk in the east, in the Western Isles of Harris and Lewis, and on the Inner Hebridean island of Islay. There are very few rivers in between that I haven't fished, not all successfully. But in almost every case my catches have been the result of knowing the right people. Their invitations have given me opportunities to fish waters which otherwise would have been impossible for me to access.

Louis Davidson

One of the first people I am indebted to was the late Louis Davidson. Louis, who ran the Balmoral Bakery and restaurant of the same name in Inverness, was a keen angler who used to take leases of the Laggan Pool and the Dochfour Beat of the Ness. He was very generous in allowing me to fish both of these stretches for a number of years, mostly in the spring before he invited corporate guests and friends to fish.

In the early 1970s, however, I was asked to act as ghillie on Dochfour and, with the late Bill Paton, we looked after Louis' guests. There were days when no guest would arrive and the spare ghillie could then fish on the finest salmon pools to his heart's content. It was on one such day that I landed my finest ever catch on the fly – 13 salmon. Oh, what memories! Sadly, Louis died in the late 1970s and the connection was broken.

Mr Herd of the Garry

Thanks to a friend's introduction, I met Mr Herd, owner of the River Garry and Loch Oich fishings, shortly after he had purchased these magnificent spring fishings in the 1970s. For a number of years, I was able to fish not only the River Garry but Loch Oich. In the spring months I landed a good number of fish each year. The average weight of my catches was always close to an outstanding 20 pounds, with the best weighing 26 pounds. Mr Herd eventually sold off these fishings and, again, the connection was broken.

Duncan Shankland

While fishing Mr Herd's water on the River Garry, I met a number of his ghillies. One of them was Duncan Shankland with whom I spent many happy days there.

Duncan left Mr Herd's employment and moved down to Dorlin on the west coast where his river was the Shiel. This short river runs from Loch Shiel to the sea, and in those days was famed for its salmon and sea trout runs.

I was invited over to Duncan's fishings several times but, by this time, the sea trout had almost disappeared. I only caught one of three pounds despite trying night fishing there on a number of occasions. But I will never forget my first day there. I had not seen the river before and imagined it to be small and fast-flowing. In preparation for the day, I had taken my thigh boots and 10 foot fly rod. Then, just in case it was windy, I also took my 14 footer. On seeing the river, I couldn't believe its size: it needed chest waders. Thank goodness I took the thigh boots and big rod.

It was late October and a beautiful sunny day. I fished with Duncan as my ghillie all morning without a touch and decided to change tactics in the afternoon. I put on a sinking line and a tiny size 12 double – Black Shrimp, of course – and, by five pm, had hooked and landed seven fish, the best of which weighed 18 pounds.

Duncan Shankland dispatches a 20 pounder from Loch Oich

I enjoyed a few more days with Duncan and, although the fishing did deteriorate, I looked forward to these trips and Duncan's company. Alas, Duncan died in 1986 and I lost another good mate.

Major Godman of Ness Side

Another great contact I made was with the late Major Godman who, in the 1970s, owned the Ness Side water on the River Ness.

At that time I was writing a weekly angling report in the Highland News – under the nom de plume Black Shrimp, would you believe? – and I used to phone Major Godman every Monday night to get the catches for the previous week. One week when I phoned him he told me that the following Saturday was free and invited me to fish then, and to bring a friend.

I had never fished that beat before and I was looking forward to it. I asked my old friend Sandy Cumming if he would like to join me and, naturally, he jumped at the chance. Sandy and I arrived at the hut on Ness Side on the Saturday morning where we met the ghillie, the late Harry Fraser, who was an old friend and an angler of some distinction, particularly on the association water. Harry's speciality was fishing the smallest tube flies you ever saw. Boy, did they work for him!

The river was in perfect ply and we were directed to the Holm Pool which was to be our beat for the day. I had recently made a 14 foot glass rod and was going to try a new Aircel number nine floating line with it. My choice of fly that day was – surprise, surprise – a Black Shrimp, but this day I was trying one tied on a size six single hook. I invariably fished doubles but that day, when checking my flies in my box, this one stood out so I tied it on.

I was soon into a fish, then another and then yet another. Poor Sandy, although I gave him an identical fly from my box he couldn't get an offer. By four o'clock I had hooked and landed seven, but it didn't matter if my friend fished in front of me or behind. He didn't have a touch.

After landing the last fish and Harry had returned from taking my catch to the larder, I was talking to him about the weight of line I was using and wondered if, perhaps, a number 10 might balance my rod better when casting. Harry told me that he had a reel with a number 10 on it and we changed over the reels. The first two casts did seem to prove that the number 10 was, in fact, a better weight for my rod, but I didn't get any more chances to try as, on the third cast, I hooked number eight. The drag on Harry's reel, however, was much too heavy and the hook was pulled from the fish's mouth. Mark you, I wasn't complaining – and never would if I could always land seven out of eight fish. That's an extremely good average.

Incidentally, poor Sandy's catch was a giant zero. Just how the day could be so one-sided, I don't know. We were using the same line and fly and casting about the same distance, yet all the takes came to my fly. It's just another of the great mysteries of angling. Major Godman, a lovely old man, became a very good friend and I fished Ness Side many more times at his invitation. But I never caught so many fish in one day as on my first visit to this lovely beat.

When in the major's gun room I had seen – adorning the walls – several beautifully painted life size salmon, all over 30 pounds, which he had caught over the years at Ness Side. On one occasion, when I was painting a life-sized cut out of a 20 pounder which a friend of another of my benefactors, Mrs Max Muller, had caught on the Beauly, I asked the major if I could borrow one of his paintings to try to copy the way in which it had been painted. He loaned me one of the paintings which was of great assistance to me.

We used to talk about fishing and shooting and I admired the wonderful collection of firearms in their glass-fronted cases in the gun room. I understood the major's wife wished to return to London and I believe it must have broken his heart to leave the Highlands. Ness Side was put up for sale and was snapped up by local businessman Hamish Campbell.

Just prior to leaving Inverness for the last time, Major Godman phoned and asked me to call at his house that evening. I arrived there somewhat bemused as to why he should want to see me. I was absolutely shaken and, believe me, totally lost for words, when he presented me with one of his salmon pictures and his Mannlicher-Schoener 6.5mm carbine rifle, which he told me he would never use again. I used this rifle many times for hind shooting. It was a beautiful weapon to use and it was only when I could not get any more of its rare ammunition that I traded it in for my modern .270.

Major Godman died not very long after he left Inverness. He was one of the finest gentlemen I have ever met and I feel honoured that I can remember him as a friend.

A real toff

I reckon that I owe Mrs Diana Boyd more than anyone for the wonderful fishing I enjoyed, first on the Findhorn and latterly on the Dochfour Beat of the Ness.

It all began in about 1950, after the family had moved up to Inverness and settled in. My dad was desperate to go camping again and, after a lot of hunting about, found a site on the banks of the Findhorn at Tomatin, between the old A9 road bridge and the railway viaduct.

That summer we transported the tents and all the other camping gear to Tomatin in the back of a lorry belonging to an old friend from Blairgowrie who dad had met in Inverness, and we set up camp. Dad was in his element but I don't think my younger sisters were all that excited about it. Naturally, I was soon trying out the Findhorn waters nearby and landed some beautiful baskets of trout. I remember one evening watching a local taking a salmon from the small pool directly underneath the road bridge. He took his fish on the worm which, at that time, I had never tried for salmon.

I didn't go back up to fish at Tomatin again, apart from a few days on the then Tomatin Hotel water where I did manage to catch two salmon one day in about 1956. That was the year after I joined the

Mrs Boyd with a fine 12 pounder from the Dochfour Beat of the River Ness

police and when I had my first car – an old Morris 8, 1938 model.

By asking around, I learned that the water I had fished when we had been camping was part of the Kyllachy Estate owned by Mrs Boyd, previously Mrs Hardy. During my years in Grahams, I had met the Kyllachy keeper Willy MacKay. Although I knew that Mrs Boyd turned a blind eye to anyone fishing the camping water, I could not, as a policeman, go fishing there without permission.

One day I drove up to Willy's house where Mrs MacKay told me that her husband was "down on the water with madam." I was shown where they were, down on the river opposite Clune House. With a bit of a hard neck I walked down through the fields to the pool where Mrs Boyd was casting a fly. Willy was standing several yards downstream of her.

I shall never forget how the conversation went. We were all within earshot of each other but Mrs Boyd said, "What does he want, MacKay?" Willy asked me why I was there and I replied, "I was wondering if I could fish the bit of water between the road bridge and the railway viaduct." Willy then repeated this to Mrs Boyd, who said, "Tell him he can go down there and help himself." After Willy repeated this to me he whispered, "Give her an hour and then come up and fish here." I said, "Thank-you very much Mrs Boyd" and, not waiting for this to be repeated, I turned and made off to my car.

I fished for trout that day without success but didn't take up Willy's offer to fish upstream and thought that would be it. A few days later, however, I met Willy in town. He told me that Mrs Boyd had said to him she was very impressed by the way I had come up and asked to fish a piece of water that everyone just helped themselves to. She had asked him, if he happened to see me in town, to tell me to phone her for a day's fishing any time.

I did that soon afterwards, of course, and so began a friendship which was to last almost 40 years. Through this connection with Mrs Boyd I was privileged to fish the finest beats on the Findhorn and the Ness at a time when these beats probably fished at their best ever. I spent many days acting as her personal ghillie. Latterly, Mrs Boyd could only fish from a boat but she and I accounted for a good number of fish together.

Unfortunately, I did not keep records of the fish I caught but had many days when I caught and killed so many fish I had to make several trips with them from the river to the car. In those days there were so many fish in the rivers that conservation did not occur to us. I doubt, however, if the stocks in the rivers were affected in any way by the number I and all other anglers caught and killed then.

Mrs Boyd had a 90th birthday celebration held for her in

Tomatin Village Hall which my wife and I attended. She managed a cast or two on Dochfour for a couple of years after that, but had to give up in her 93rd year. Sadly, shortly after that the grand old lady passed away. I have so many happy memories of her and will never forget her. She was a real toff!

Mrs Max Muller

I suppose it would have been in the early 1970s when, through a mutual friend, I met Mrs Max Muller. This fine lady and her husband spent a great part of their year in Jersey but, after they bought Benula Estate near Cannich, they spent more of their time up in the Highlands.

Mr Max Muller was very keen on stalking and it transpired that his good lady just happened to be interested in fishing. Courtesy of the late Jock Gibson (see My Sherry Fish), I had previously stalked hinds on their estate which, incidentally, was reached by boat at the west end of Loch Mullardoch. This came up during conversation when we first met and I was invited to come up there to shoot some hinds. I subsequently spent many very happy days there learning from stalkers Jimmy Jack and Murdo Urquhart a lot of the skills required to become more proficient at this game.

I recall one day when Mrs Max Muller accompanied Jimmy and me to the west end of Loch Mullardoch. Leaving her in the boat, we began to climb the extremely steep slopes of Bein Fhionnlaidh, a small Munro of only 3,298 feet, in search of our hinds. All went well and Jimmy obviously knew where he was going. But it was all that I could do to keep up with him although he was a good 20 years older than me. We stopped just at the crest of a rise and Jimmy assured me that there would be beasts "just over the other side of this crest. Get your breath back before we get in close enough to have a shot." Then the mist came down

Ghillie Bill Paton nets a salmon for Mrs Max Muller at Burnmouth, on the Dochfour Beat of the River Ness

and, within a couple of minutes, we couldn't see five yards ahead of us. We lay there for a while hoping the mist would lift but it was down for the day. At one point I could actually hear the deer breathing and the sound of their feet in the heather. They could only have been about 20 yards from us, but I could see nothing!

By this time I was completely disorientated and lost, and thanked the Lord that I was accompanied by someone who had some idea of where we were. We gave up thinking about stalking any more and I followed Jimmy as he led me – sometimes uphill? – until more than one and a half hours later we came right down the hill directly above the boat where a very anxious Mrs Max Muller was looking around hoping for us to reappear. I think Jimmy must have had a built-in SatNav for his knowledge of the hill in zero visibility was incredible.

To say that I was hungry was an understatement, not having eaten since a plate of cornflakes at six am at home before I left to drive to Benula. The flask of coffee and sandwiches I had left in the boat were life savers and I felt so much better after eating and drinking. We returned to the dam end of the loch and, again, Jimmy's ability to find our way home in almost dark conditions was remarkable. I had many other days stalking at Benula. The sport was excellent and I even managed to take my eldest son Grigor there to shoot his first hind.

Mrs Max Muller was much keener on the fishing side and took beats on the Beauly and Glass every year. At that time I had never fished the Beauly, but eventually fished every pool from Beaufort Castle down to the road bridge. My catches, all on the fly of course, were remarkable by present day standards. It was a poor day if I did not catch more than two or three salmon.

For several year Mrs Max Muller took a lease of Dochfour and, like Mrs Boyd, invited me to fish there. Boy, was I spoiled then!

Unfortunately, both Mr and Mrs Max Muller passed away a number of years ago. I consider myself to have been extremely lucky to have known this fine couple whose friendship and generosity I will never forget.

Joyce Ross and the Tay

Joyce Ross was the sister of well-known Inverness ironmonger Gilbert Ross. I first met her in the late 1960s through the late Willy MacBean, who introduced me to trolling on Loch Ness. Joyce, then a lady in her 60s, was very keen on fishing and used to enjoy a day out on the loch.

She told me that her sister had a bungalow on the banks of the Tay at Grantully and invited me to go down there to have a cast. Naturally, I was very keen to do this and it was arranged that, while I was there, I would stay with the boatman – I would say ghillie – Tom Hay. That far upstream, the Tay at Grantully is narrower than the Ness. I went down on perhaps half a dozen occasions and seldom failed to catch a fish.

One of the best days I had there, which has a remarkable sting in its tail (see The day I met Miss Ballantyne), I was fishing a pool at Little Ballinluig accompanied by Tom. I hooked a good fish on a three inch black and orange devon – the Inverness Special as Tom called it. When it was played out Tom did the necessary with the net and I admired a lovely clean run 14 pounder.

I carried on fishing and was very soon into another fish which I realised was even bigger. It took a long time to play and I soon had quite a gallery, formed by the occupants of several cars which had stopped on the nearby road to view the action. The fish, a magnificent 24 pounder, was safely landed and we were standing admiring it when the driver of a Rolls Royce among the parked cars came down the bank and spoke to Tom, who he obviously knew.

He told Tom that he was fishing the Caputh beat on the Tay the following day and asked Tom if he would act as ghillie for him. Tom told him that he could not as he was employed on the Grantully water. He then introduced me to the visitor – who I shall call Mr L – and suggested that I might be the man for him.

Mr L asked me if I could ghillie for him and said, "You can fish as well." I needed no further prompting. A chance to fish another Tay beat? – yes please!. We arranged to meet in the farmyard of Caputh Farm the next morning. (See The Day I met Miss Ballantyne).

Had it not been for Joyce's generosity in inviting me down to fish at Grantully, I would not have enjoyed the wonderful sport I had there and the events described in the following chapter would never have come to pass. I still remember with great affection this lovely lady who so much enjoyed the outdoor life.

9

The day I met Miss Ballantyne

I pulled into the farmyard beside the bridge over the Tay at Caputh well ahead of the time I had arranged to meet Mr L, for whom I was to ghillie that day. I had never seen this stretch of the Tay before and quickly ran up to the bridge to check out the pool where, in addition to my duties as a ghillie, I hoped to fish later that day, as promised by Mr L. The river seemed to me to be in perfect ply. I likened it to my favourite Ness pool, the MacIntyre, although much wider.

I returned to the farmyard and assembled my spinning rod. Shortly afterwards two Rolls Royce's pulled into the farmyard, making my little Austin A40 look right out of place. Mr L got out of his Rolls Royce and introduced me to the two men who got out of the other car. One was a retired Admiral and the other gentleman was a South African. I put up their spinning outfits, noting that all had Hardy LRH spinning rods with Abu Ambassadeur 6000 reels – the best money could buy. I tied on three inch wooden devons of different colours from a stock of my own make I had taken with me.

Mr L asked, "Where do you think we should fish, ghillie?" Based on the pool's vague similarity to the MacIntyre, I suggested that Mr L and I should go up the left bank (looking upstream) and the other two rods should go up the right bank.

Mr L and I crossed the bridge and made our way up the bank towards the neck of the pool. It was then that Mr L said I couldn't fish as only three rods were permitted on the water. To put it mildly, I was rather upset and disappointed. I had given up fishing a perfectly good beat further upstream, where I had caught two fine salmon the previous day, to fish this new beat as promised. I felt Mr L had not played the game with me. I didn't say a word although I admit I was fuming!

I had never previously used a multiplying reel and it was pretty obvious that neither had Mr L. His efforts at casting were rather pathetic and he said that the reason for this was that my lure was too light. He insisted on putting a spiral lead on the line above the lure. While I admit he could cast it further, on almost every retrieve the lead snagged the bottom resulting in a lost lure and lead on virtually every occasion.

Mid way through the morning, one of the rods on the other side of the river hooked and landed a nice fish of about 16 pounds, but at lunch time that was the only fish hooked. As we were preparing to go back across the river to the hut for lunch Mr L said to me, maybe having a twinge of conscience, that I could have a cast. Believe it or not, on my first cast I hooked and landed a nice nine pounder. I didn't have another cast!

On the way back over the river to the hut, all I could hear was Mr L saying, "I cannot understand it. I have been fishing all morning without a touch and he has just one cast and gets a fish. I can't understand it." At lunch the four of us were sitting in the hut, which has a window facing upstream above the bridge, when Mr L said to me, "Do you know who stays in that cottage there?" He pointed out a cottage on the bank of the pool half way up from the bridge. Of course, I had no idea who stayed there and said so. He told that that it was Miss Ballantyne, the lady who held the record for the heaviest salmon caught on rod and line in Britain. I knew of Miss Ballantyne, of course – what salmon angler didn't? When Mr L asked me, "Would you like to meet her?," I just couldn't believe my luck and said, "Yes."

Mr L and I walked up to the cottage which had a porch outside the front door. He knocked and shouted, "It's Mr L, Miss Ballantyne" and I heard a reply, "Come in." On entering the cottage I saw this little old lady sitting in a chair wrapped in a blanket. I was introduced to her and, after exchanging a few pleasantries, Mr L and I returned to the hut. I was thrilled to have met this grand old lady – something to tell the boys when I got home!

Mr L asked me where he should fish in the afternoon and I replied that we should return to the same place. He agreed but said there was something he had to do first. We both went back to his Rolls Royce and, when he opened the boot, I saw something I had never seen before or since. The back of the cavernous boot had been fitted out with the most beautifully made wooden cabinet stretching from side to side and floor to top. There were many drawers in this cabinet, some large and some small, and one on the top was the whole width of the boot. He first opened this long drawer and from it brought out a brand new Hardy rod identical to the one he had used all morning. From another drawer he took out an Abu reel identical to the one he had used that morning. He said to me, "John, I'm going to change my tackle to change my luck."

I had never seen anything like that, but I changed over the rods and reels and tied on yet another of my wooden devons. This time, however, I put some lead wire on the mount and told him that this should give him more distance and there would be less likelihood of snagging on the bottom as often as he had been doing. We crossed the bridge again and went up to the neck of the pool. When we arrived there, Mr L said I could have another cast and – honest! – I hooked another salmon on my first cast. This one weighed 10 pounds.

I could not fish on, of course, and I spent the afternoon standing alongside Mr L offering encouragement and advice. The leaded devon was working very much better than the spiral leads and snags were certainly less frequent than they had been in the forenoon. After countless blank casts I saw the tip of his rod bend and jerk and I yelled at him, "You've got a fish." He replied, "No, it's the bottom again." But when the rod was almost pulled from his grasp he realised that, indeed, it was a fish! After a long tussle during which the fish pretty well did as it pleased, I managed to put the net under a real beauty of 22 pounds. That put a smile on his face!

By then it was five o'clock and we all made our way back to the farmyard where I dismantled the rods, put all the salmon in basses and packed everything into the cars. Before driving off, they all shook my hand and Mr L said, "If you wish to fish on, please hand any fish you catch into the keeper's house," vaguely indicating uphill in the direction of the village of Caputh. No tip was offered by any of them!

As soon as they disappeared I ran back across the bridge, up the pool and began spinning, but after half an hour I hadn't had a touch. The fish had gone off. I couldn't believe it! Returning to my car, I quickly assembled my fly rod. I had a number five silk line and tied on a two inch Parker Major tube fly in a Shrimp pattern, a fly with which I had been particularly successful on the Findhorn. Unfortunately, these flies do not seem to be on the market now. They were great spring and back-end flies.

I began fishing at the bottom half of the pool where I could wade out with thigh boots just far enough to facilitate my Speycasting. Within a few casts I got a long slow draw and I was into a fish. This eight pounder fought well and was landed without too much trouble. I continued fishing and almost immediately connected with another eight pounder which was landed without incident.

With the potential for much larger fish I realised that without a gaff or net I was taking a bit of a chance. I remembered having seen a gaff hanging in the porch of Miss Ballantyne's cottage. After putting the two fish into the boot of my car, I called at the cottage. My knock on the door was answered by a shout, "Come in." As I went in, Miss Ballantyne said, "Oh, you look cold." (It was raining with a cold upstream wind.) "Go through to that cupboard and pour yourself a dram and put the kettle on. We'll have a cup of tea."

I did as I was bid then sat down and had a long blether with her as we drank the tea and I finished the dram. Naturally, I asked her all about the 'big fish'. She told me that she had been fishing with her father in a boat, in the pool right outside her cottage. They had been harling (pulling baits behind the boat as it was rowed from side to side in the pool) when one of the baits had been taken. They had "quite a tussle" (that is an understatement if ever I heard one) with her father taking charge of the boat while she took the rod. I cannot remember how long she told me it took to land the monster, but they were about half a mile downstream before it could be gaffed. It weighed 64 pounds and is still the largest salmon ever caught by rod and line in Britain.

I was particularly interested in what she caught it on and she told me it was taken on a natural gudgeon (a small freshwater fish) mounted on tackle similar to sprat tackle. I'll bet not many people knew that!

I was now feeling nice and warmed up, thanks to the dram, tea and the fire, and told Miss Ballantyne that the reason I had called was to ask if I could borrow the gaff I had seen hanging in the porch. She said of course I could borrow it, and that it would be of interest to me to know that it was the very gaff her father had used to gaff 'the fish'. Just to hold that gaff was in itself quite exciting – to think that I was actually handling a piece of angling history! It was a hand-forged steel gaff attached to a five foot long staff and bound with copper wire. I wonder where it is now?

I thanked Miss Ballantyne for her hospitality and quickly ran back across the bridge and up the pool to where I had caught the eight pounders. I stuck the gaff in the grassy bank a bit below where I intended to begin fishing and quickly got my line out and started casting. Within a few casts I got this really long hard pull and I was into another fish!

I knew immediately that this fish was something out of the ordinary. Right after hooking it, it began running upstream, steadily but not that quickly. The problem was that, no matter how much extra strain I put on, it made no difference. The fish just kept going upstream. My four inch Hardy Perfect reel was loaded with a 30 yard Kingfisher number five silk line spliced to 150 yards of backing. None of all the salmon I had ever hooked and played had run me so far. Indeed, for the first time since I had put the backing on the reel I could see the knot to the drum spindle coming into view. In order to try to prevent the last few inches of line being stripped off the reel, I got out of the water and ran upstream, attempting to wind in at the same time.

Despite this, the fish kept running slowly but surely upstream. Just when I thought that a broken line or cast was inevitable, the fish began to drop back downstream ever so slowly. With almost 180 yards of line out there was a huge belly on the line which must have been exerting a terrific drag on the fish. It seemed to take forever to reclaim even the backing on to my reel. It was only after the splice was safely back on the drum that I got my first look at the fish. It was huge!

After a few short runs and a lot of splashing about, it eventually turned on its side exhausted and floated down nicely to within range of the gaff which I picked up easily from the bank. With the first attempt, I gaffed it cleanly just in front of the dorsal fin and heaved it up well clear of the water. It later turned the scales at 32½ pounds, my heaviest salmon ever!

Being a greedy sort of fellow, I went straight back in and, would you believe it, immediately hooked another. I had a quick look at it before it fell off. It was, in my opinion, every bit as big as the one I had just landed. By this time it was getting late. After returning the gaff to the cottage, I set off on the drive home to Inverness. Do you know, no matter how hard I tried I could not find that keeper's house!

Canada – an angler's paradise

Dingwall Gaelic Choir, with which my wife sings, was invited to sing in Vancouver in May of 1991. When I heard about this invitation, my immediate thought was, "I could go fishing over there while they are singing." It was arranged that Anna and I would travel to Canada with the choir and many followers and, with thanks to many contacts, I fixed up fishing for three days during the time the choir was performing.

I knew from research that May was too early for some of the five species of Pacific salmon. There was, however, the possibility of catching Chinook in the ocean and spring-run Steelhead in some of the rivers. It was arranged that I would be a guest at Black Fish Lodge for three days. I would fly from Vancouver to Port Hardy, at the north end of Vancouver Island, where I would get a taxi to the village of Port MacNeil, situated on the east coast of Vancouver Island facing the west coast of mainland Canada. From there I would take a float plane to Black Fish Lodge.

The long flight to Vancouver from Glasgow via Toronto passed very quickly. It was almost one long ceilidh from the minute we took off until we eventually landed at Vancouver. Just how some of the singers could keep going so long without sleep beats me, but it did help to pass the time.

I only had a couple of days before I was to set off on my greatest ever adventure but Anna and I, accompanied by our friends Peter and Mary Home and Janet and Willy Fraser, crammed in as much sightseeing of that beautiful city as we could. Then, after bidding

Anna cheerio, I left her and the rest of the choir at their motel and set off in a taxi for the airport – and into the unknown!

The flight from Vancouver to Port Hardy was uneventful but the views of the Pacific and the rugged west coast of the Canadian mainland were breathtaking. After a short drive to Port MacNeil I got my first look at my transport to my eventual destination. It was a Beaver float plane. I had, of course, seen many of these on film but never in the flesh, so to speak. Soon I was sitting alongside the pilot as we taxied out from the jetty and took off across the smooth waters of Vancouver Sound towards Canada's mainland. We didn't fly higher than a few hundred feet and followed the line of a huge inlet which led us alongside and over a multitude of tree-clad islands until our destination came into view.

Black Fish Lodge is a floating log cabin anchored close to the north shore of Kingcome Inlet. I turned on my camcorder to record the faultless landing and smooth approach to the cabin where we were met by the owner and Pat, who was to be my personal guide during the next three days. After the introductions I was asked to change into fishing togs. Within an hour of arriving I was aboard a 20 foot glass fibre boat going out to fish.

The method to be employed was deep trolling with a downrigger. This was a completely new experience to me. The bait was to be a herring with its head cut off at an angle. It was mounted in another manner totally new to me, with three single hooks embedded in line along the length of the fish. A kink was put in the tail which made it spin lazily when pulled through the water. The line was attached, with a quick release clip some 20 feet above the bait, to a cable just above a 10 pound lead weight. The weight and the line were wound down to the appropriate depth or to where the sonar showed lying fish. The boat then slowly followed the coastline of Wakeman Sound with the baits trailing behind.

This was not unlike my previous experience of trolling in Loch

Ness but I must admit that this has never been my favourite branch of angling. Sitting on your bottom waiting for a fish to take is not tactile enough for me. By early evening that day we had not made contact with any salmon, but the day was not without its compensations. Our boat passed a group of what I thought were big seals – which my guide told me were actually Californian Sea Lions – and I saw several sea eagles and two otters. I felt I had arrived!

Returning to the log cabin, we had a beautiful meal and, after a dram of Old Inverness I had taken with me (for medicinal purposes, of course), I went to bed. It was a very strange experience to lie in bed and hear the water lapping on the deck below. But that didn't prevent me having a good night's sleep.

The next morning I was up at six am. After a quick breakfast Pat and I set off in the boat. About an hour later we arrived at a jetty close to the mouth of the River Wakeman where it entered the ocean. There we were met by a real character, Steve and his dog Muttley. This chap lived in his log cabin near the jetty all year round and passed his time acting as a guide to fishermen or hunters. That's what I would call a really lonely existence! I was interested to know that among the prey the hunters shot were grizzly bears, which I was told were common in this remote area. I asked the boys what steps I should take should I have the misfortune to encounter a grizzly. Their answer was, "Big ones!"

On a more serious note they explained that if I had the misfortune to encounter a grizzly, I couldn't out run, out climb or out swim one. The only advice they could give me was to lie down and pretend I was dead! Fortunately I never did see one. As I had been advised I made plenty of noise when out alone on a river bank. I don't think I have ever given so many noisy renditions of "I Belong tae Glesga" in my life as I bank fished over the next couple of days.

Anyway, back to Steve. We loaded a rubber dingy on to the back of an old truck and he drove us about 10 miles up an old logging road until we reached a broad pool. After unloading the dingy we arranged for Steve to meet us at the Three Mile Pool later in the afternoon.

The river was extremely high and very coloured. Although I fly fished most of that day I had no luck. We drifted down the river in the dinghy and went ashore to fish from the banks of likely looking pools. I don't think I have ever been so anxious when, while drifting downstream, Pat said, "Hold on Jaan, here come the rapids!" I was holding on with one hand on each side of the dinghy and trying to keep my bottom off the floor of the craft in case we ran over a submerged log. All this time I was being pitched side to side and front to back. Obviously I survived and here to tell the tale, but boy, that was hairy! After all, the bottom of the dinghy was only a sheet of rubberised canvas and that would have provided no protection at all.

Steve picked us up and we returned to his cabin where we had a cup of coffee well laced with some brandy. Pat and I then went back on to his boat and, for the remainder of the day, we pirked with large, heavy silver lures. The depth we were fishing in was in excess of one hundred feet but it was absolutely wonderful sport. We each landed three Chinook salmon with an average weight of around 15 pounds. Believe me, they really gave a good account of themselves and we returned to our cabin well satisfied. After our meal and a dram, it was back to bed.

The following morning we were up bright and early again and made our way directly to Steve's where he took us many miles up to the Wahpeeto River, a tributary of the one we had fished the day before. This river was also in spate but, unlike the Wakeman, it was running clear. It was not unlike the Findhorn in character with some deep pools and fast running sections.

Incidentally, this river is fed from a glacier on Silverthrone Mountain. Again we drifted down and fished the likely pools from the bank. I fly fished and spun this river with large Black Shrimps and spoon lures with no success.

Eventually my guide said that steelhead, which were our prey, had a very small window of vision and unless I placed a lure directly in front of their noses I was unlikely to have a take. He suggested I try something different and kitted me out with a large cork float on my line. For bait he tied up a large single hook and a plastic lure which was the same size as a ripe raspberry and looked not unlike that, but was orange in colour. It was meant to represent a cluster of salmon eggs.

At home I had used a similar rig for worm fishing for salmon and soon got the feel of it. I had to guess the depth of the water to be fished and adjust the float so that the bait would just about hit the bottom. I must be a really lucky guy for I hooked and landed two big steelhead which were both returned after very long hard-fought battles! We estimated that they weighed around 14 pounds and 20 pounds respectively. I also caught a three pound rainbow trout which was also returned.

By lunch time we had drifted down to the pool on the Wakeman where I had commenced fishing the previous day. It had cleared up a lot and looked very fishable. After trying the fly with no result, I decided to give the spinner a go. I tied on a gold-bladed Flying Condom and within three casts I was into a hard fighting fish. When I landed it, Pat told me it was a Dolly Varden char of about three pounds.

As far as species were concerned I was doing well, having landed four. A few casts later, when I hooked and landed another 'never seen one before type,' Pat told me that it was a cut-throat trout (similar to our sea trout). I caught a couple more of each species on the same lure and he asked me what it was called. I told him that it was known at home as the Flying Condom. He replied, "Oh, safe fishing, eh Jaan!" That was the end of that day's activity and we returned to the log cabin well satisfied with the day's sport. Salmon was on the menu that night, washed down with a wee dram of Old Inverness and then to bed.

On the third and last day my plane was arriving to collect me around one pm. Clearly, I had to be ready, all packed up, before then. We had the usual early start and returned to where we had pirked at the end of the first day. We pirked away for about four hours and again our bag was pretty even with four each. My biggest would have been about 20 pounds. As we had killed a sufficient number earlier in the week for smoking and eating as our evening meal, all these were returned to grow heavier.

Returning to our base and packing away my tackle and clothes, I was ready to return to Vancouver. In my luggage were two of my first catch of Chinook which had been smoked "on board". The plane arrived on time and I bid a farewell to my first Canadian fishing pals who, unfortunately, I will never see again.

After the flight back to Vancouver I joined up with my very understanding wife. On our final night there I wore all my tartan finery and attended the final Mod Concert where I listened to the best of the performers who had competed during the week and drank a few drams in appreciation of their efforts.

Although the fishing rods had been put away, the holiday was not over. Anna and I, together with Peter and Mary Home and Willie and Janet Fraser, went on an awe-inspiring holiday travelling through the magnificent Rockies. At the end of each day we gathered in one of our bedrooms for a nightcap and this was accompanied by biscuits and freshly smoked 'John Cathcart caught Chinook Salmon' – the perfect end to a perfect day!

I thought that this would be my one and only trip to Canada but in 2000 my fishing pal Bryan Allely said, as we were both now retired, we should arrange a fishing trip to Canada before we got too old. I was more than keen, of course, but had my doubts that my wife would agree. Much to my surprise, Anna was in total agreement. But where could we go? Canada is a very, very big place!

I was aware that the MacGruer family from Foyers have a sister Cath who is married and living in British Columbia where members of the MacGruer clan often went to fish and came back with stories of monster fish. There is no knowledge like local knowledge and thus began a flow of phone calls between Inverness and Terrace BC where Cath and her husband Brent Smith live. Brent just happens to be a 'Canadian fishing nut' and we had lots in common to talk about. Brent and Cath offered to put up Bryan and me in their home, but I felt that was a bit of an imposition and asked them to fix bed and breakfast for us at some local establishment.

The holiday was finalised and in late July of that year we flew from Glasgow via Calgary to Vancouver. We spent a couple of nights in Vancouver seeing the sights, China Town and Gas Town to name but two. We got about by taxis and I noticed that if the driver didn't have a turban, he was black or of Oriental origin. Vancouver certainly is cosmopolitan.

As arranged, we flew to Prince George where we stayed overnight before taking a train to Terrace. The airport is quite some distance out of the town and we took a taxi. This taxi driver was white and apparently knowledgeable about angling and we enjoyed a good chat during the journey. As he dropped us at a motel I mentioned to him that he was the first Canadian taxi driver we had seen since our arrival in Canada. He replied, "I'm from Germany!"

The following morning we caught the train and our carriage had a little French-Canadian conductress on board. She made the journey very interesting by relaying the driver's comments such as, "If you look out the left side of the train you will see a bear" or some other animal. As the train passed a large lake which the conductress told us was named Fraser Lake, the train stopped and all the passengers got out to enjoy a 20 minute break strolling on the golden sandy beach of this lovely water.

We duly arrived in Terrace where we were met by Cath and Brent. They welcomed us like long-lost family members and took us directly to a pub known as The Back Eddy where a gang of Cath and Brent's pals had gathered to meet the guys from Scotland. Their welcome was typical of those we had from everyone we met, in the street and in shops. As soon as they heard we were from Scotland, that was it!

Bryan and I were then taken to a large house eight miles out of Terrace where we were introduced to Bill Penner and his wife, our hosts for the next three weeks. After I hired a car we called at one of the local fishing tackle shops where we met the proprietor Dave who had arranged for us to collect a set of chest waders each. Then Cath and Brent took us down to the local river, the Skeena, which is glacial blue in colour. About 20 rods were fishing in line no more than 30 feet apart at the head of the pool. Each was fishing a powerful single handed fly rod and casting upstream, obviously with sinking lines and hand-lining furiously.

We were told that the fish, lying in shoals facing upstream, do not actually take the fly. When the fly, moving downstream, comes in line with their mouths, opening and shutting as they breath, it foul hooks them in the mouth. I reckoned I had never heard so much nonsense in my life, but by the end of our holiday I really believed that this was a fact.

Any amount of fish were heading and tailing below the line of anglers and I made a mental note to fish there the next day when, by Speycasting with my 15 foot rod, I would be able to cover at least three times as much water and fish than the other anglers. Who knows how well we might do?

Brent then directed us about 30 miles to Kitimat, a hydro electric town, where a river by that name runs. The river was high and very coloured but many anglers, including children in their early teens, were coming away from the river, each carrying at least one fish. These fish were all about 12 to 14 pounds and quite coloured. They had vertical lines down their flanks and Brent told us that they were Chum or Dog salmon. All had been taken spinning.

Next morning, after a huge breakfast of pancakes, maple syrup and crispy bacon served by Bill, Bryan and I made our way to the Skeena pool. But after flogging the water below the line of anglers, a high percentage of whom were Germans and Italians, we didn't get a touch. During that time, however, at least half a dozen fish, all apparently Sockeye weighing about six pounds, were landed by the line so we decided to change rivers and headed to Kitimat.

The river had cleared a lot and was not dissimilar to the Ness – no blue water and you could see to wade. Barbless single hooks are mandatory and I had tied up a good selection of these prior to the trip. I tied on one of these, a Black Shrimp, I think in about size two. Bryan and I were soon in action and each of us landed several fish to about 16 to 18 pounds. All but one of these were Chum salmon, but I caught a Chinook of about eight pounds, a very small one for that species. We were both fishing floating lines with about ten yards of fast sinking line on the point. We did foul hook a few fish which, in the now clear water, were obviously very plentiful. You could actually see the shoals.

That was the beginning of a marvellous fishing holiday. We didn't catch fish every day but we fished in places where, without Brent, we could never have done so. One of these places really sticks out in my memory. Brent worked for a timber company and one day he and his pal Kevin Derow drove us 70 km up a newly opened logging road where they were abstracting timber with an average age of 250 years from an area where timber had been growing for 10,000 years. It was highly unlikely that anyone had ever fished there before.

Eventually we stopped at a wide passing place and could see the blue-coloured River Kiteen several hundred feet below us. The only way to get to the river was to slide down the steep shale embankment formed by the road cuttings. We all managed to get down without incident and then found that we had to get across to a small island in order to fish the pool on the other side of the island.

Brent was the only one wearing waders and he piggy-backed first Kevin and then me across to the island. When it was Bryan's turn Brent was either exhausted due to his previous exertions or he simply stumbled, but the end result was that they both ended up neck deep in the water. Unfortunately, I didn't have the camera ready! It was a very warm sunny day and it didn't take long for their clothes to dry once they took them off and hung them over tree roots abandoned on the island by floods.

Meantime, Kevin and I crossed the island where I saw a narrow pool which was almost a replica of one of my favourite Findhorn pools, the Pullochaig at Shenachie, except for the colour of the water. The pool was maybe 15 yards wide by 40 yards long and looked fishable for its whole length. The far side, for most of its length, was against a sheer rock face. I fancied trying the fly in the manner I would use at home and tied on a size two fly. Kevin opted for salmon eggs as his bait and he geared up with a float in the same style I had used when I had caught my steelhead on my first Canadian trip.

We both began fishing with me starting first. Kevin floated his bait past my line when it was close to my bank. After fishing it to the tail of the pool he wound in and went up behind me and again floated the eggs past me to the bottom of the pool. On about his third run down he struck a fish. I wound in and then filmed the action, most of which was well below the surface. After a strenuous tussle he brought a 25 pound Chinook to the shallows where, with the use of a pair of pliers, he removed the 5/0 single from the fish's mouth and it shot back into the pool.

I decided 'when in Rome…' and quickly set up my spinning gear with float, size 5/0 single and a cluster of salmon eggs. I began to fish the pool down, as Kevin continued to do, and on several occasions I felt a sharp tug. I was obviously striking far too slowly as Kevin explained it was essential to strike fast when float fishing with salmon eggs.

The next time I felt the line tug I struck as fast as I could. This time I was on! The fish kept deep most of the time I played it. Kevin filmed the action and I eventually managed to bring the fish ashore where, after unhooking it and taking more photographs, I returned a Chinook around the 25 pound mark. But these Chinook were very coloured as, Kevin told me, they had probably been in fresh water since about April.

I then tried one of my Aswood devons, a two and a half inch fluorescent orange Tiger with a single hook mount, and quickly landed another two fish, both around the three pound mark. One I recognised as a Dolly Varden char but the other was not unlike a brown trout except for its shape. It had a thinish body and a head almost like a pike. I was told it was a Bull trout – another species to add to my tally.

The big problem with this river was that the pools were few and far between and access along the river bank was almost impossible because of natural tree growth and flood debris, so no more fish were taken. The climb back up to the road was exhausting, to say the least, but on the way home I was amply compensated when no fewer than five black bears crossed the road, staying directly in front of our vehicle. I managed to film most of these, some of which were as close as 20 feet to where I stood. I will always remember the reaction of one bear as I said "Hello there bear" while filming just outside the open door of Brent's crew carrier – ready to jump back in if the bear made any attempt to come any closer to me. It turned round and gave me an almost contemptuous look before turning and shuffling off, apparently without a care in the world!

Another memorable day, although not for the fish caught, was when our host Bill Penner accompanied and directed us to a large gravel island on the River Skeena which he named 'Chinaman's Bar'. (He had seen a Chinaman fishing there!). This island was at least six hundred yards long and littered with many trees and other flood deposits. The main part of the river, some 20 miles downstream of Terrace, was over 100 yards wide at the far side of the island which was easily reached after wading across a shallow stream close to the side of the roadway. We soon crossed over the island where Bryan and I began fly fishing while Bill chose salmon roe as his bait.

After quite a while without an offer between us I decided to change to a spinner and put on the 2½ inch fluorescent yellow Tiger with which I had had some success earlier on the Kiteen. I didn't have a touch but on one occasion, after retrieving the lure to within a few feet of where I was wading and lifting it out of the water to make another cast, a beautifully marked fish swirled just where the lure had been. I immediately identified the fish as a Dolly Varden of about four to five pounds, but it didn't come again despite many more casts in the same area.

While all this was going on I could see activity down at the bottom of the island. I could make out two figures moving about between what appeared to be a windbreak and the water's edge. I was sure that more than once I saw splashing close to where they were. Curiosity got the better of me and, as there wasn't much happening where we were, I went down for a nosey.

When I got down to the couple I found that they were middle-aged Italians who, although they told me they had been in Canada for 39 years, still spoke with a very strong Italian accent. I introduced myself and told them I thought I had seen them landing fish. They said they had actually caught four that afternoon – three steelhead and one Coho, all of which had been returned.

I was more than anxious to know what method they were using and asked if they would mind if I watched what they were doing. They were more than happy to show me. They had a 10 to 12 foot rod, very powerful like we would use for boat fishing, and an Ambassadeur 7500 reel filled with line which I guess would have been about 60 pounds breaking strain. (Bear in mind that Chinook to over 80 pounds are caught regularly on the Skeena!). The line was tied to a three-way swivel to the side eye of which was tied a short length of lighter nylon attached to an eight ounce triangular lead. The remaining swivel eye had a metre length of nylon attached to it and at the end was a lure known as a Spin Glow with three orange beads above a barbless 7/0 hook. I would describe the Spin Glow as a ping-pong ball with fins attached to make it spin. The lures float and are finished in a range of colours.

My new friend then cast the whole caboodle maybe 12 to 15 yards out into the river. After winding in the slack line and checking that the reel tension was to his liking, he slid the rod butt into a plastic tube which was anchored upright in the gravel. He then hung a small copper bell on to the top ring of the rod before he and his wife sat down in their windbreak to await

Lorenzo's fish – a 20 pound steelhead on the River Skeena

developments. Do you know, I hadn't been speaking to them more than a couple of minutes when I was interrupted by a ting-a-ling. A fish was on! Lorenzo ran across and picked up the rod from the tube and handed it to Maria who began to play the fish. It wasn't long before a beautiful clean run steelhead of about 20 pounds was brought into the shallows and Lorenzo, without touching the fish, quickly unhooked it using a pair of long-nosed pliers, and it was gone.

By pure coincidence I just happened to have a triangular eight ounce weight and an identically coloured Spin Glow with me, courtesy of Bill's tackle box. After setting up this rig on my much lighter rod and reel, I asked Lorenzo if he would mind if I fished in front of him. He had no objections and I cast out my rig about 20 yards downstream of him. Clearly, the lead anchored itself to the river bed with the lure spinning above and downstream of it. I just stood there holding the rod and waited and waited, but nothing happened. I then thought that I had a far better idea. I let the lure fish in one position for about a minute then drew it in about five yards, let it lie there for another minute and repeated the procedure until the lure had to be recast.

I continued with this cast, stop, retrieve, stop method until my concentration was interrupted by another ting-a-ling from Lorenzo's bell! This one was yet another fine steelhead of about 12 pounds. I went up to watch the action and after it was unhooked and released I decided to go further upstream to try my new technique there. It was when the bell rang yet again that I decided it was late in the day and time to head back up to join my mates upstream. I honestly believe that my method must be more successful than the totally static method employed by Lorenzo and his wife, as the lure must be presented to more fish per cast. Unfortunately, it was nearly the end of our holiday and I didn't manage to test the method again. I would have loved to have managed another visit to 'Chinaman's Bar'.

I am equally certain that this method, although a mite boring, would work on our rivers in Scotland if only the river beds were like where I was fishing in Canada – clean, flat beds of small gravel which did not snag the lead. From my experience our river beds are not quite like that as my accumulated losses of lures over the past years would testify. But if anyone is prepared to lose countless leads and lures, give it a try!

The whole holiday was a truly wonderful experience which I will never forget. I managed to land almost every species available. The one exception was a Coho salmon, a species which had just begun to run at the end of our holiday. Oh for another week there!

Canada is without doubt an angler's paradise but, as I found, local knowledge is a great asset. I would love to have managed a third trip so I could take advantage of the little knowledge I feel I now have. That's not possible now but boy, do I have a shoal of memories!

Riverside buddies

There is great camaraderie among anglers. Over a lifetime of fishing I have met and befriended many people, unfortunately far too many to name. Without their company on the river bank a day's fishing just wouldn't have been the same.

Real faith

One of these gentlemen – a very special one – was the late Sandy Cumming, brother of Tommy Cumming who, until he stopped fishing recently, was in my opinion one of the land's finest fly fishers. Sandy and I shared many happy days on the Garry, Oich and Ness and between us had some great catches and experiences.

Sandy was a good bit older than me and, in the late 1970s, was approaching his 70th birthday. One of the places he fished regularly in the spring, courtesy of the late Louis Davidson, was the Dochfour beat of the River Ness. When he went fishing there he cycled from home up to the Laggan Pool, at the bottom of the Dochfour beat, and then walked up the river bank to Dochfour waters, a total distance in excess of three miles.

I will never forget one evening, about nine thirty pm in April. As I was about to leave home to go on night shift, there was a knock on the door. When I opened it I saw Jimmy Smart, a fellow angler and a close friend of Sandy, standing there. Jimmy told me that he had received a phone call from Sandy's wife saying that he had not returned home from fishing. Jimmy didn't have a clue where to start looking for Sandy and had called on me to see if I had any idea where he might be! A 70-year-old, fishing alone, and it had been dark since seven pm – what more would you need for beginning to think the worst might have happened?

I phoned my colleagues at the police station to tell them that I would be late in for work and asked for someone else to brief my shift. I also said that I might be requiring the services of the police van, two officers and a stretcher. This was in the days before mobile phones, of course. If the worst was found to have happened I would have had to make my way to the nearest house, a mile downstream of the Laggan pool.

I asked Jimmy if he had thigh boots in his car and he had. I put my waders into the back of his car and, armed with powerful torches, we set off for the Laggan. We drove to the hut at the pool where we parked the car. After putting on our waders, we walked upstream towards Dochfour. At the end of the path at the top of the Laggan Pool we saw Sandy's bicycle propped against the fence. My heart fell and I began to fear the worst!

We continued upstream to a backwater at the bottom of Dochfour's Culbuie Pool where I began to shout, "Sandy! Sandy!" at the top of my voice. I repeated this several times as we continued upstream. Then there was a faint reply, "Is that you John?" I was so relieved to hear Sandy's voice as I thought he must have fallen and broken a leg, or something debilitating like that. I shouted, "Hold on Sandy, we're coming."

Jimmy and I ran as fast as we could up the river bank until our torches illuminated Sandy. He was not lying curled up on the bank as I was expecting but standing upright with his fishing rod fully bent facing the river. He was into a fish! The first thing Sandy said was, "I knew it would be you John. Thank goodness you've arrived. I've had this fish on since half past five." The time then was well past 10 pm.

My relief at finding Sandy alright was replaced by curiosity. How big must this fish be? Sandy had a gaff, which he passed to me, and

I got Jimmy to shine his torch on the water while I waded out and guided my hand down the line until it entered the water. As I got Jimmy to redirect the torch to that area, I could see this big (not huge as I thought it must be) salmon with the devon lure hanging at the corner of its mouth, almost stationary beside my feet. I quickly gaffed it, lifted it clear of the water and waded ashore. When administering the coup de grâce with the gaff handle, I noted that there was no sign of the hook. It had fallen out as I gaffed it!

The fish turned the scales at 28 pounds – a big fish certainly but I really believed that he must have hooked a real monster to have had it on for five hours. The major factors were the darkness and that the banks of this pool had no gravel beaches or shallow parts at which to land a fish in the dark. Sandy had just held on! He said to

Yet another good fish taken by Sandy Cumming – a 26 pounder from the River Ness

me afterwards, "I knew that if I hung on long enough John would come and give me a hand." Now that's what you call real faith!

This is, without doubt, one of my most favourite fishing memories.

A successful partnership

One of my closest fishing buddies was the late Steve Fraser Jnr who I first met on the Inverness Angling Club stretch of the River Ness in about 1960. We really hit it off together and shared many days fishing and, during the close season, evenings and days making flies and experimenting at making minnows.

Steve's father and several of his contemporaries had, for many years, annually fished the River Dionard in the far north of Scotland at

Steve Fraser Snr plays a salmon on the River Dionard

Durness, where they always stayed in the Cape Wrath Hotel. I was introduced to this river by Steve and we stayed in the same hotel, then managed by Miss MacKenzie. This was the first hotel I had ever stayed in and my main recollection of it is the large number of monstrous brown trout – caught in the nearby limestone lochs – displayed in cases on the walls of the bar, lounge and dining room.

Steve and I fished the river for several years, catching a fair number of late run fish up to about 14 pounds and some nice sea trout from the shore in the estuary below the hotel in early summer. We also fished the Findhorn round about Glenferness for a couple of years and had a few memorable days there.

But it was on the association water of the Ness where we probably caught most fish. In those days the runs of summer salmon were prolific and we often fished as a team. If Steve was fly fishing, I would spin the pool. If we both chose to fly fish, he always fished The Sweep and I used my then favourite Shrimp pattern. On days when we both thought that spinning was the best bet, I would use a Toby spoon and Steve would use a black and orange devon.

I will never forget an August morning around 1963. We met up at the Rossie Lodge side of the MacIntyre Pool at about six am. The river was in perfect ply with all the beats of every pool being fishable. There were many other rods out before us including, of course, the club president Charlie 'Scout' MacKenzie. As on every morning, Charlie had probably been there since daybreak. They reckoned that if you were out on the MacIntyre Pool before Charlie – also known as The Resident – you couldn't have gone to bed!

Several fish had been landed before Steve and I arrived, and Steve opted to fly fish the bottom beat while I went to the top of the next beat upstream and decided to spin as no other rod on this side of the river was using a spinning rod.

Steve Fraser Jnr, with whom I enjoyed a great friendship and successful fishing partnership

Steve was soon into a fish at the bottom of the pool. I put on an 18g Zebra Toby, my then favourite colour of this lure, and very quickly hooked and landed two lovely clean-run eight pounders. When I went down to help Steve land his second fish, one of the other rods there, Dougie Miller, asked if he could borrow my spinner as he had only brought his fly rod.

After gaffing Steve's fish, his second eight pounder, I returned to where Dougie was still spinning away with my outfit. He asked, "Just three more casts John?" Would you believe it, with the third cast he hooked and I subsequently gaffed yet another eight pounder for him.

Nothing more was taken from the MacIntyre Pool for the next hour or so and Steve and I left and made our way down to the Legion Pool, just below the suspension bridge (at that time the main bridge over the Ness). The ebbing tide had just left the pool, which I always reckoned was a good time to fish there. We both spun down the pool and I caught a real beauty of 18 pounds, also on the Toby. We then made our way back upstream to the Ness Islands where we went to a seldom fished pool known as The Pass, where Steve's devon added to his tally with a 10 pounder.

We then took a well-deserved tea break and, about four pm, decided that the MacIntyre would be worth another look and made our way back there. We both concentrated on the fly for the remainder of the day and rounded off what must have been one of the most productive days in the club's history with another three each. Not bad for club water, eh? I often wonder just how many fish were running up the river in those days to give us such sport.

Steve and I continued our friendship for, unfortunately, only a couple more years, but in that time we had some really wonderful days fishing together, mostly on the Ness but also on the Findhorn and Glass.

We were also exploring the manufacturing side of lure making and spent a great deal of our spare time in each other's garages and houses thinking up new ideas and producing prototypes. But all this came to a most abrupt halt when, during the evening of 9th September 1965 while on duty alone in the CID office in Inverness, I received a call to attend the shooting of a young man at an address I immediately recognised as Steve's.

After first collecting a colleague, the late Detective Sergeant Evan Lumsden, I called at Steve's home where, on entering the hallway, I saw the body of my pal lying at the bottom of the stairs with blood all over his chest. Lying nearby was his single barrelled shotgun. I just could not believe that I had been speaking to him just a few hours earlier, at lunch time that day, and had arranged to call at his home at the end of my shift at 9.30 pm. I had to get on and do my job, including taking photographs and interviewing witnesses. It was, without doubt, the most difficult time I ever had in the police. We will never know exactly what happened, but the last time I had spoken to him he had asked if I fancied going out for a shot at the geese the next morning. I had declined but said I would see him that evening.

It was quite a while before I could make the effort to go fishing again but one evening, while I was in that particular mood, I took out my fly-tying kit and pondered what fly I would tie. Steve's favourite fly was The Sweep and mine the Shrimp, so I thought about combining the features of each to make a new fly. The Sweep, as the name implies, is black and the predominant feature of the Shrimp is its long tail. So the Black Shrimp was born, in memory of my old pal Steve Fraser.

I reckon that some of Steve's magic was passed on to this fly for I have since caught many hundreds of salmon on it. For a number of years its popularity, particularly on the Ness, outstripped most others. My best outing with the Black Shrimp was 13 in a day at Dochfour and my best tally on the club water was 51 in three weeks. The Black Shrimp serves as a fitting memorial to a great friend and a top class angler who I will never forget.

Black Shrimp dressing

Hook size	*12 to 2 double or treble*
Tag	*5 turns silver wire*
Tail	*Long fibres of black cock hackle or, in larger sizes, of black squirrel tail*
Rear half body	*Yellow floss ribbed with silver oval tinsel*
Middle hackle	*Orange*
Front half body	*Black floss ribbed with silver oval tinsel*
Cheeks	*Jungle cock, one each side at top*
Hackle	*Long black cock hackle*
Head	*Black varnish*

The vision of Blind Malcolm

After I fully retired in 2000, I often went into Ormiston's Tackle Shop (now bought by J Graham and Company, Castle Street, Inverness) at their premises at the top of the Market Brae Steps and spent a great deal of time, as you do in that kind of shop, just blethering.

Jim, Danny, Gavin and I would put the world right on an almost daily basis and it was during this time that I heard the name 'Blind Malcolm' for the first time. I had not previously heard of this chap and, although he was described to me, I still didn't know him. I learned that Malcolm Campbell had been keen on becoming a gamekeeper all his life. Unfortunately, he had lost his sight a few years earlier as a result of diabetes. Rather than let this hold him back, it appeared to have had the opposite effect and he was still very active.

One day when I was just standing about in the shop, a lady came in followed by a man wearing a fore and aft, dark glasses and carrying a long white cane. From the banter which immediately began between him and the staff I realised that this was Blind Malcolm.

The lady left the shop and a five-way conversation began between the staff, Malcolm and me about how the fishing was doing, and other sporting matters. At no time whatsoever during this conversation was my name uttered by any of the staff and I was completely dumbfounded when, after perhaps seven or eight minutes into the conversation, Malcolm turned to me and said, "Are you still fishing Dochfour, John?" I didn't know what to say. How could he possibly have known it was me, as not once had my name been mentioned during the previous conversation? I answered that I no longer fished there as, unfortunately, all my contacts had passed away. I think I left the shop shortly after that.

A few days later I was doing stand in duty in the shop for one of the boys who had a hospital appointment and I answered the phone, saying in my most posh voice, "Ormiston and Company, can I help you?" The caller, whose voice I recognised as Malcolm, asked if he could speak to Jim Hunter and I just couldn't resist replying, also in my most posh voice, "Oh, I'm sorry. No-one by that name works here." Malcolm's reply was, "Oh, stop mucking about, John."

I met Malcolm in the shop a few more times over the next few weeks and one day he asked Jim and me if we fancied a day's rainbow trout fishing. We were all for it and Malcolm said he would fix up the day. When Malcolm left the shop, Jim told me that the day's fishing was to be at Phones Estate near Newtonmore where Malcolm had been working before he lost his sight and where there was a stocked loch. I had heard of the loch and that it was renowned for its big trout.

The day was duly arranged and, after picking me up, Jim drove to Malcolm's where we collected him and his gear. We then set off with Malcolm in the front and me in the rear. On the hour-long journey, Malcolm turned to me and asked if I had wondered how he had known it was me in the shop that day. I told him that I had been at a complete loss as to how he had known. He then asked if I could remember – in 1984, before I retired from the police – giving a talk to gamekeepers on the laws pertaining to poaching.

I had been the force Poaching Officer and I recalled giving several such talks about that time. Malcolm told me he had recognised my voice from one of these talks. That in itself was more than remarkable but he also gave a physical description of me at that time – six foot tall, curly hair going grey, slim build and wearing a grey jacket, dark trousers, white shirt and blue tie. That exactly described me and the clothes I wore at the time. I was astonished!

We carried on to the loch, which I had never seen before, and Jim and I set about putting up the rods and tying on the casts. Malcolm insisted that Jim tie on "that big orange fly" to his cast. After preparing the tackle, we had to go down a very steep bank to the jetty where the boat was tied up. I took hold of Malcolm's arm to lead him down but he insisted that I walk down normally while he placed his hand on my shoulder and just followed me.

We had decided to do a bit of bank fishing before taking the boat out and I helped Malcolm into the water, which was about knee deep at the edge, and handed him his rod. Before he began to cast, he asked me, "Where is that birch tree, John?" I saw a birch tree some 20 feet to our left, told Malcolm where it was and he began casting away. During our spell of bank fishing, both Jim and I hooked up on the bank behind, but Malcolm didn't once.

After a while trying this – when Jim was the only one of us to hook and land a fish, a beauty of 10 pounds – Malcolm and I took the boat out. I was directed to all the hot spots on the loch. "Just behind that wee island where the burn comes in," then "At the side of that weed bed." He certainly knew the loch and it was difficult for me to accept that my companion was totally blind!

We had a most memorable afternoon. Malcolm and I talked about fishing and shooting, and recounted tales of past events. And the fishing was good as well! Malcolm landed five trout up to about four pounds in weight to my two. But one of mine weighed just under 10 pounds, my heaviest ever rainbow, and Malcolm netted it for me. I brought the fish to the net but Malcolm instinctively knew just when to lift it out of the water. Not once did I have to unfankle Malcolm's cast, although mine required to be sorted out more than once that day. To sum it up, I don't think I ever spent a more pleasant day out in a boat. Malcolm's attitude to life was an inspiration and not once did he mention his blindness. It certainly was no handicap to him.

At about five o'clock we tied up the boat and, after dismantling the rods and packing the car, we set off for the house of keeper Michael Glass to square up for the day's fishing. It was then that Michael told us that something terrible had happened in America. It was the 11th of September 2001 – a date that none of us will ever forget.

I never saw Malcolm again. His health deteriorated and, on the 16th of December that year, he passed away at his home in the presence of his family. He was only 34 years old. My regret is that I only knew Malcolm for such a short time. His sense of humour was unbelievable and any worries you may have paled in significance compared with his. Yet his attitude to life was an example to us all. He was a delight to have known and I feel the better of my all too brief contact with him – like all the other people he met, I'm sure. He certainly rates as one of my favourite fishing buddies.

"Come away ma wee Geordie!"

Richard Chilton Young and I first met when I joined the police in 1955. Always known as Dick, he came from Bradfield, Essex, and had served in the Gordon Highlanders at Fort George barracks. It was during his time at the fort, and while attending dances in Inverness, that he met his wife Rhona. After his demob they married and settled in Inverness where, in 1948, he joined Inverness Burgh Police.

As a rookie, I was often paired up with Dick and he taught me a lot about the job. He had an incredible knowledge of the Highlands and I soon learned that he did a lot of deer stalking on estates near Inverness. I had been in the police for about a year when Dick asked me what tackle he would need to fish for salmon on the River Glass. I had never fished that river but was aware that it was the upper reaches of the River Beauly. I told Dick that if he arranged the day I would provide the fishing tackle.

The day was arranged and Dick drove me up to Upper Glassburn, then owned by the late Captain William MacKay. The river, which is hydro controlled, was difficult if not dangerous to wade because of the height of the water that day, and was more suited to spinning. I provided Dick with a spinning outfit and set up one for myself. The lures we used, I recall, were made of lead, 2½ inches long and painted red and gold. I hooked and landed nine fish, all about six to eight pounds, but by late in the day poor Dick hadn't had a single offer.

I walked up the bank to where Dick was fishing at the tail of the pool. He said he would have one more cast and then we would call it a day. He turned to cast and, as he did so, his left leg slipped and went into a hole in the bank. He fell on to his back and the lure, instead of going across the pool, went high up into the air and plopped into the water not five yards out from the bank. "You'll not catch fish that way," I said to Dick. But, would you believe it, after Dick stood up and wound in all the slack line, there was a fish on! That was Dick's first ever salmon and the first day I caught more than two in a day.

I fished the Glass and Conon with Dick many more times over the next few decades and had some wonderful days sport with him. One day, when we were fishing the Conon, I was using a 12g copper Toby which the fish seemed unable to leave alone. After landing about half a dozen and Dick had not been able to make contact with one, despite changing lures, I told him that the copper Toby seemed to be the lure to use. Dick went through his bag and came out with an 18g copper Toby which he tied on. Believe it or not, Dick did not land one fish that day and I finished with 19 – the most I ever caught in a day! Pheromones? I can hardly believe that the different sizes of the lures made all that difference.

An old friend, Fred Hartley, who I fished with several times and who usually caught fewer fish than me, had a theory. I generated electricity in my body which was transmitted down the line to the lure. The fish detected this electricity and had to grab the lure. I wonder, is that the secret?

Dick and I shared very many happy days together fishing on different Highland rivers, and during these days many funny things happened which made us laugh then and many times later when these incidents were recounted. One of these occurred when we were fishing the Glass together. I had overcast my minnow and hung it up in the bushes on the other side of the river. There was an old rowing boat tied up on our side and Dick volunteered to row across and free the lure. The river was running very high but he soon reached the other bank and unsnagged the lure which I quickly wound in. My companion then began the return journey and, when he was about mid stream, I just couldn't resist shouting, as he strained on the oars, "Come away ma wee Geordie," thinking of the similar phrase shouted in a recent film starring Bill Travers.

At that precise moment, one of the rowlocks – which was a hazel stick – snapped and Dick ended up lying on his back in the bottom of the boat with his feet in the air. This was quite hilarious to watch but actually far from funny, as Dick had lost one of the oars. I will never forget poor Dick paddling furiously downstream with the single oar until he caught up with the lost one. With great difficulty, he managed to bring the boat to our shore and, with my help, back upstream to its original berth.

Another incident involving Dick was when he and I, and another work colleague, Dougie Jack, were fishing the River Ling, near Dornie. This is a small spate river and we were worming. Most of the pools are very overgrown and didn't lend themselves to fly fishing. None of us had been to this river before and we were exploring it as we made our way downstream. We came to a pool below a waterfall where the banks on either side were about 20 feet high. Dougie and I went downstream to where the pool widened and was fishable from the bank but Dick, standing above the waterfall, dropped his worms into the pool below. There was no access from the waterfall to where Dougie and I were as there was a solid clump of rowan and birch trees growing on the bank. It was quite a ridiculous situation. If Dick did manage to hook a fish from there, how was he going to land it? I voiced my concerns to Dick but, stubborn fellow that he was, he just brushed them aside.

Several minutes later Dick shouted that he was into a fish and I thought, now what? He played the fish, a nice 10 pounder, for a few minutes and then, when the fish was becoming tired, reality struck Dick. How was he going to land this fish? He began to force his way through the almost impenetrable jungle with his rod held high above his head. While doing so, he obviously had to leave the fish to its own devices. I saw his line drifting down towards the tail of the pool, and I just couldn't resist it. I cast across Dick's line, pulled it ashore and then played it by hand. With Dougie's assistance, I landed the fish which was dispatched and unhooked. I then threw the hook back into the water. Meantime, there was the sound of breaking branches and a lot of

Sweet memories – Dick Young at the oars

huffing and puffing going on above us. A good 10 minutes later, Dick finally emerged from the tangle of foliage and began to wind in his slack line. What he said when he found that the fish was no longer there I will not repeat, nor can I tell you what he said when I held up his fish and asked, "Is this what you're looking for, Dick?"

A rather amusing incident took place when Dick and his son Dennis, also a keen angler but much more into stalking like his dad, took place when they were fishing the Laggan Pool way back in the 1970s. While fly fishing, Dick hooked a grilse and duly landed it without too much trouble. But things took a peculiar twist when he was unhooking it. It was not his fly that was in the fish's mouth! Further examination revealed that Dick's fly was further up an alien cast, hooked into the loop of the cast. The likelihood of this happening is millions to one. The poor fish, which some other angler had hooked and lost due to not properly tying his knot between line and cast, had been left to swim about trailing at least eight feet of nylon behind it until Dick's fly came along and caught the loop of the cast. Poor fish, lucky Dick.

Incidentally, Dick told me at the time that, if anyone heard about this incident and wished to reclaim his fly, it was about 20 feet up the second tree upstream of the hut on the Laggan Pool! Oh what sweet memories! Dick died suddenly in 1998, aged 70, and he is sadly missed.

Taking the Mickey

Born in Sunderland, Bryan Alley moved to Inverness in 1967 to work as a rep for Unilever in their bakery, fats and oils division, visiting bakeries throughout the north of Scotland, Orkney, Shetland and the Hebrides. I first met him in the early 1970s and we hit it off immediately through our common interests in fishing and deer stalking.

I introduced Bryan to my contacts on the Findhorn at Shenachie, where we took a week's lease every year from Mrs MacKintosh of MacKintosh, and at Coignafearn, where my friend Frank Stuart was then the head keeper. Together, we fished for both brown trout and salmon for about 30 years and enjoyed some wonderful days sport there. The best day I recall Bryan having was the day I shot my stag there (see 'My MacNab'). He took 10 fish, the best weighing 24 pounds (I gaffed it), all on a trout rod and his own dressing of a fly he called the Allely Special.

Bryan had his own contacts, both in deer stalking and salmon fishing on the Spey. He introduced me to Bill Brailsford who was the head keeper at Garragie, near Whitebridge, where I enjoyed many wonderful days shooting hinds with Bill and Bryan. These are among the memories I will always cherish.

Perhaps one of the best of the contacts Bryan introduced me to were London-based Cyril and Rae Woods, and Alec and Charlie MacDonald. I was invited to join their syndicate, of which Bryan was also a member. We fished the Brae Water of the Spey, near Fochabers, every May where, for the first few years, the fishing was very good. But it dropped off and catches fell so low that if one of the party managed to catch one fish for the week we were doing well. About this time Cyril passed away and father and son team Mike and Mark Lambert joined the gang.

Back end fishing on these beats had the potential to be prolific in terms of catches, but we could see no prospects of getting a lease at that time of the year- until fate stepped in. At the Highland Field Sports Fair at Moy that year I took a stall to sell my devons and flies. My fly tier, Carol Thomson, who was tying flies to customer orders, and Bryan were giving me a hand. He served a gentleman who purchased a number of Black Shrimps and, in conversation, Bryan asked where he was going to use them. The gentleman replied that he was going to fish on the

Brae Water beats of the Spey. We told him that was where we fished in the spring but we couldn't get a lease in the back end. The man then identified himself as the new factor for these waters and told my pal to write and ask about a lease there.

Bryan with a good catch from the Brae Water of the Spey

The end result was the syndicate got a lease, first on the Brae Water beats and then on the Castle Water beats. We enjoyed fantastic sport until the early 2000s when the catch rate dropped drastically and the rents increased to such a level that I, and the majority of the other members, decided that it just wasn't viable and reluctantly gave up our lease. Isn't it just typical? – a year or two later the catches began to improve, but we were out!

We also fished together on the River Oich for about 20 years in the spring and enjoyed some wonderful sport both with salmon and, from April onwards each year, with brown trout. We used to experiment with sinking lines and nymphs and did very well with these.

In the late 1990s, while fishing on the Oich, my friend said that now we were both retired we should think about going to Canada for a fishing holiday. Having already tasted Canadian fishing when I had gone over there with my wife and Dingwall Gaelic Choir, I was all for it but didn't expect my wife to be too enthusiastic about the idea. I didn't broach the subject with Anna, as I fully expected a rebuttal. When Bryan and I were fishing the next week, I voiced my concerns that Anna wouldn't be too keen.

"That's not what she told me," said Bryan. "She's fully in favour of it." I raised the subject with Anna when I got home and she told me, "Go and get it over with, or I'll never hear the end of it." That meant "Yes" to me so Bryan and I began to make preparations to travel to Canada in July of that year. By that time most of the species of fish we hoped to catch should be in the rivers.

I was aware that well-known Foyers angler Alla MacGruer has a sister, married to an angler, in northern British Columbia and that he and other angling-mad relations often went over to visit and fish there. I felt there was no point in going out there and then beginning to look for places to fish, so I contacted Cath and Brent

Smith at Terrace BC. They arranged accommodation for us and we flew out from Glasgow via Calgary to Vancouver laden with cases, cameras and rods. We must have encountered very sympathetic airport staff for neither of us was charged for excess baggage.

There followed one of the most memorable fishing trips I have ever enjoyed. Bryan and I, who were referred to as the guys from Scotland, were treated royally by Cath and Brent and all their friends, and the cheery welcomes we received from everyone we met were most heart-warming. The fishing was not at all bad either. We both caught a good number of fish of every species of salmon except one, the Coho. And there were some big ones!

I always carried a camera and camcorder and got some fine footage of Bryan landing fish. And he filmed me doing the same. One day we were making our way from the River Kitimat back towards our car. As we were going through a dense wood Bryan, who was walking slightly ahead of me, suddenly stopped and said, "John, there's a moose." I immediately dropped my rods, pulled my camcorder from its case and switched it on. I had seen a dead moose at the side of one of the roads, but to get a close-up of a live one was really something. I looked around but could see nothing. I asked Bryan, "Where is it?" He pointed to the ground just in front of him and, when I looked, I saw this tiny mouse with huge round ears sitting there. A 'Mickey Mouse!' We have had many a laugh about that since.

I have shared more shooting and fishing experiences with Bryan than with anyone else and he is, without question, one of my best fishing buddies.

Faithful friends

Last among my fishing buddies, but certainly not least, were two great pals with whom I shared about 20 years of friendship, companionship and devotion. They were my inseparable shadows,

Ilé I retrieves a trout

the black Labrador bitches Ilé I and Ilé II. Ilé is Gaelic for Islay, the inner Hebridean island which is my wife's birthplace.

I first met Ilé I when I called at the Culloden home of Anna, my wife-to-be, in 1982. All of us hit it off from the start. Ilé was aged six at that time and, as Anna's daughters Mairi and Alison were at school and Anna was at work, the dog spent some time in the house on her own. I worked shifts so was able take the dog out wherever I was going almost every day.

Ilé I and I thoroughly enjoyed each other's company, she doing what dogs do, running about freely, meeting other dogs, animals and people, and being able to sniff away at things to her heart's content. When I went fishing I took her with me and I think I witnessed her first introduction to the water. Boy, did she enjoy that! I also found that she just loved to pick up and carry trout for me – without damaging them – and her services as a courier were very convenient, especially when trout fishing in a river like the Findhorn. I had only to unhook the fish, kill it and throw it to Ilé and she would follow me down the pool carrying the trout. On reaching the bottom of the pool, I could retrieve it and put it in my bag or have her carry it back to the car.

Ilé had a very happy life, going out almost every day and quite contentedly sitting in the car when I had to make long journeys. As long as I stopped regularly for her to have a sniff and let her do her business, she was happy. I'll never forget, when returning home from a long journey – from Wick, for example – she would lie asleep in the car until I turned the corner of our street, when she would sit up and become quite excited. Was it the scent of the area she recognised?

She enjoyed very good health all her life and was seldom at the Vet, but at the age of fifteen and a half she became very tired and incontinent. With a very heavy heart I arranged for the Vet to call at our home and, as I held and spoke to her, she was put to sleep. Anna couldn't stay at home while this was happening, but the least I could do was to be with her at the end. I buried Ilé at the top of the garden, where she loved to sniff around, and erected a small headstone there. For ages after that, when out fishing or driving, I would speak to her or turn around expecting to see her still there. I missed her so much! There would be no more dogs, said Anna, and I reluctantly agreed.

While fishing at Ness Side every summer, I met Peter and Annie Taylor from Rutland, who were tenants of the beat, and we became good friends. They regularly stayed overnight with us and they kept inviting us down to their home for a weekend break. But at that time Anna was working in Raigmore Hospital and, as she didn't get many weekends off, we were unable to accept their offer.

In 1994 Anna left Raigmore Hospital and began working as a district nurse auxiliary on the Black Isle, and didn't then work weekends. The break was arranged and we set off on the long journey to Rutland in April of that year. Anna's daughter Mairi was working in Carlisle then and had just moved into a new flat, so Anna put some old sheets and towels in the car to use for cleaning the flat. We spent a very pleasant evening in Carlisle and the next morning set off for Rutland. Mairi said she didn't need the cleaning cloths, as she had plenty, so they were left in the car.

The journey to Rutland was uneventful and we were soon pulling up in front of Peter and Annie's lovely cottage at the end of a lane known as Pudding Bag Lane. They welcomed us at the gate with their two Labradors eager to meet us, jumping excitedly. I then saw a tiny black Labrador puppy bobbling up towards the gate. Thinking that this was an addition to their family, I said to Peter, "Another dog Peter. I thought two would be enough." He didn't reply.

When we entered the garden and had exchanged greetings with our hosts and the two adult dogs, I was very surprised when Anna, who is not really a doggy person, bent down and picked up the puppy. I was even more surprised when she turned and handed me the puppy and said, "This is for you John." It was the week of my sixtieth birthday and this was a surprise birthday present for me! I was absolutely gob-smacked and didn't know what to say. When I was asked what I was going to call her I could only think of one name – Ilé.

So began my second companionship with an animal. Her character was unique and we bonded very closely. This gift explained all the old sheets and towels which, incidentally, were not required on the journey home. Ilé II slept on either Anna's lap or mine all the way home, except for a stop at Carlisle to show her off to Mairi.

Once I got home I found that Anna had arranged with our friend George Macdonald to erect a small shed which was to be our new dog's kennel. But as he had creosoted it I could not put the dog in it for several weeks, until the fumes had dispersed. I made a temporary kennel under an old table in the garage for that night and for the next few weeks. I warned all the neighbours that we had a new dog in case she disturbed them during the night, but Ilé II didn't whimper once, then or ever after. She took to sleeping in the garage, and later in her proper kennel, without any trouble at all. It was only in the last four years of her life that we took her into the house at night during the winter months.

Like her predecessor, Ilé II became a constant companion and accompanied me on numerous fishing trips to the Ness, Oich, Findhorn, Spey and Nairn. On a couple of occasions, when she was still quite young, I lost her and it was only after returning to the same spot the following morning that I found her lying, apparently waiting patiently for me, in the exact place where I had last seen her. In both these instances I had been wading deeply and believe that my scent had been carried away by the current and, as she couldn't see or smell me, she had wandered off looking for me. But she returned and waited at the very spot where she had last seen me.

Ilé II became quite a favourite, particularly on the banks of the Mill Stream Pool on the Ness where she would lie patiently in front of the bench where anglers were taking a break, hoping a sandwich crust might fall or be thrown towards her. She was seldom disappointed.

Sadly, Ilé II developed a heart condition and bad arthritis in her joints. In August of 2006, as the poor lass was in constant pain with no hope of improvement, I took her to the Vet. Even as she was being examined, her tail was thumping against the table legs.

With Ilé II and a good catch from the Castle Water of the River Spey

She was so happy, even then! We were told that the best that could be done was treatment which might extend her life by a month or two. Very reluctantly, from a selfish point of view, I agreed that

Ilé II be put to sleep. She was twelve and a half years old.

I don't mind admitting that I cried more than I ever believed I could as I cuddled Ilé II's head and spoke to her as the Vet administered the injection. I had Ilé II cremated and scattered her ashes on the waters of a private part of the River Nairn where we often fished together.

I stood there for a long time watching the grey film slowly spreading down the pool and thought back to the many happy times we had spent together – watching her chasing rabbits through the sand dunes on Islay and swimming alongside me as I waded chest deep across a deep stretch of the Spey to reach an island from where I intended to fish.

I do miss both my old companions and it is a certain fact that I will never forget them. I would love to have another dog but this is totally impracticable as I can no longer walk and exercise one. But my son Grigor recently acquired a Husky pup and I go over to his house regularly just to see how it is developing. This brings back many happy memories!

12

A day on Loch Coulin

In the late 1960s I was invited by Gordon Cameron, along with my late pal Steve Fraser's father of the same name, to have a day on Loch Coulin. I had no idea where it was or what fish it held, but my research soon revealed that it was one of two then famous sea trout lochs which lay in the head waters of the Loch Maree system. The catch there was, of course, sea trout with the occasional salmon and I could hardly wait for the day to come. I prepared casts with all the appropriate sea trout flies such as Black Pennel, Blue Zulu, Silver Invicta and Soldier Palmer. I could go on forever naming the flies which were all guaranteed to be killers there.

The day, about the beginning of September, arrived at long last. There had been a lot of rain which I was told would help the fish ascend the River Garbie from Loch Maree to Lochs Clair and Coulin and, providing we got a good breeze, prospects of sport looked good. Gordon picked up Steve and me and we began the long journey into Wester Ross. This was an area which I knew little about then and seeing the rugged mountains of this part of the west of Scotland for the first time was quite exciting.

Having reached Kinlochewe – after the stunning descent of Glen Docherty, set against the backdrop of Loch Maree – we turned left on to the Torridon road and, for a few miles, followed the tumbling waters of the River Garbie which was in spate. We turned left again and soon saw a small loch at the head of the river which I was told was Loch Clair. After passing it we crossed a bridge over a strip of water joining Loch Clair to a larger loch which I learned was Loch Coulin, our destination for the day.

After getting out of the car and kitting up, I tied on one of my pre-prepared casts comprising a Black Pennel on the bob, a Silver Invicta on the middle dropper and, because I always liked a tail fly with a bit of silver in it, a Butcher on the point. All these hooks would have been size eight.

Gordon had fished the loch since the 1950s with his father and other friends, including Hamish MacPherson, of MacPherson's Sporting Stores which used to be in Inglis Street, Inverness; Alan Conon, an Inverness chemist; and many other Inverness businessmen keen on the sport. Gordon knew the various drifts and lies well.

The loch was a lovely size. It didn't take too long to row across to the opposite shore after a drift. We took it in turns to row while the other two fished. There was a nice southerly breeze but sport wasn't exactly brisk at first. Gordon was first off the mark with a fish of about three pounds and quickly followed it with another of the same size. Steve was next to hook a fish, another fine sea trout just on the four pound mark. I was beginning to think that it just wasn't my day but, just before going ashore for lunch, I at last saw a swirl at my flies and hooked a fish. This one, typical of most sea trout, ran, ran and ran before leaping clear of the water, shaking like a leaf in the wind, before plunging back into the water and racing towards me. I furiously wound in the slack line and was mightily relieved to find that the fish was still on. By now it was exhausted and was soon expertly netted by Gordon. My six pounder had taken the Butcher.

There was another boat on the loch that morning with three men on board. Gordon told me that one of the rods on it was the late Sir Godfrey Style, a one-armed angler of some distinction. I was somewhat amused to see that when the boats passed in close proximity, he would raise one of his oars upright in a salute to us. I had never seen that before, or indeed since, but I think it was a nice gentlemanly gesture between fellow anglers.

After lunch the breeze dropped and we spent most of the afternoon chasing breezes. Despite having several rises to our flies, we didn't manage to make contact with any more fish. It was about then Gordon suggested that, as the River Garbie was in flood, some of the large pools just below Loch Clair might be worth a cast. So we tied up the boat, put our gear back in the car and drove down to the river with me holding the three rods out of the car window.

Arriving at the top of the river, we began to fish downstream and that afternoon we had a great time, each landing two trout with an average weight of close to 2½ pounds. All of mine fell to the Butcher.

Unfortunately, that was my only visit to this charming little loch. The surrounding mountains – Beinn Eighe, the Liathach and Sgurr Dubh to the north and west and Sgurr Ruadh to the south – made it one of the most striking locations in which I have ever fished. It is a great pity that the decline in west coast sea trout stocks has affected this and most other fisheries. I can only hope that, in the not too distant future, there will be a rethink and change in the policies regarding fish farms in the sea close to the mouths of traditional sea trout and salmon rivers. In my opinion, sea lice are the main killers of migrating sea trout and salmon smolts. Hopefully, when this is resolved, a drift down the north shore of Loch Coulin will once more produce rises from sea trout and set a few hearts a-flutter!

On a happier note, a week or so after my trip to Loch Coulin, Gordon Cameron again visited the loch. Using a Soldier Palmer, he hooked and landed, with the assistance of his wife Hilary, a magnificent fish of 15¼ pounds. It was assumed, because of its size, that it was a salmon and, after photographing, it was cut up and shared among friends. But an examination of the photograph showed all the tell-tale signs – square cut tail, spots below the lateral line and the mandible of the mouth being in line with the back of the eye. It was a sea trout, the biggest ever recorded from this delightful loch!

13

A visit to Harris

During my time in the police, when annual leave was allocated on a rota basis, my 1971 summer holiday fell the week after the kids went back to school. I was hoping to take a fishing trip with my eldest son, Grigor, and recalled one of the constables on my shift – Norman MacMillan, a 'Hearach' (native of Harris) – often telling me that the fishing on his island was in a class of its own.

I asked Norman if, through his contacts, he could arrange some fishing for me over there during my holidays. A little while later he told me that the "best" he could do for me was a day on Amhuinnsuidhe Estate. The day allocated to me was the Friday at the end of the holiday week. I was very keen to take Grigor, then aged 11, and arranged for him to be excused from returning to school for another week.

On the Monday of that week we set off on our adventure. Neither of us had ever been on a ferry and we spent most of the journey to Stornoway standing on the deck in glorious weather admiring our first views of the Western Isles. Accommodation had been arranged in Tarbert with 'PK' Morrison, brother of Chief Inspector D A Morrison in Stornoway (see Poaching) and his wife Mina who both looked after us Royally during our stay.

We spent most of the early part of the week just exploring the island, fishing various lochs hoping to catch some brown trout. But a long drought and extremely low water levels were probably the reason for our lack of success. One day we drove down to Rodel where I met the late John MacCallum, the proprietor of the Rodel Hotel, and sampled a dram of Royal Household whisky which only a select few premises in Britain are entitled to stock.

Upon hearing how poor our fishing had been, John suggested that I drive north, up the east side of the island, until I came to a place known as Quidnish and try fishing a loch there. We left Rodel and were soon at the loch he had described. After fly fishing and spinning there without an offer, I began to think that all I had heard about the great fishing on Harris was so much hot air.

There was a tiny stream running from the loch to the sea, a mere 50 yards away, and I decided to have a spin in the salt water to see if I could perhaps hook a saithe. The tide was full out and the rocks I had to stand on were all coated in seaweed. There was also a floating band of weed about 10 yards wide against the rocks and I had to cast over that before I could reach the open water. I tied on a silver Toby spoon, which I felt would be an appropriate lure, and was casting away without success when Grigor shouted that he had seen a salmon jump and pointed behind me. I quickly cast in that direction and after about four turns on the handle I got a sharp tug. I struck and a lovely silver fish, immediately recognisable as a grilse, jumped out of the water with the Toby hanging out of the side of its mouth. A salmon in salt water – that's a first, I thought!

I played it out for a few minutes until it became tired then considered how I was going to land it The only way was to get it on top of the weed and try to slide it over until it was close enough to grab. All seemed to be going according to plan as I got the fish about half way across the floating weed. Then the hooks came out. The fish, well out of reach, began flapping and trying to force itself down through the weeds, but they were too thick. I tried to hook it with the Toby but all I could catch was the weeds. I then tried another method. I held the lure and, holding the rod out as far as I could in front of me, I tried to throw a loop of line over the fish until, at last, the loop went underneath its gill cover and I was able to pull it ashore. My first Harris salmon weighed five pounds.

I tried fishing from the shore at different locations round the coast of Harris but the only other catch I made was a pollack of about four pounds, also on the silver Toby, off a rocky point at Kyle Scalpay. If I had checked out these fishing spots properly, and taken the state of the tide into consideration being trying them, I might have done better, but I admit that I was a complete novice in that field.

While fishing at Kyle Scalpay I met a gentleman – the local postman if my memory serves me right – who offered me the use of his rowing boat. I jumped at the chance as this gave me an opportunity to fish further out from the shore. I was mindful of the very strong currents which run between Harris and the island of Scalpay and did not venture too far out from the Harris mainland.

Lying in the bottom of the boat were two mussels which the postie had left after his last fishing trip. I used them to bait up the bottom hook of my rig, and Grigor's, before dropping them over the side and letting out line until we hit bottom. Within seconds we got bites and on striking and winding in we each landed a good-sized haddock.

Unfortunately, we had no more bait with which to tempt more haddock and I told Grigor to continue fishing by jigging his white feathered rig. I decided to change to a lure which had brought me success fishing out from Ullapool. It was a chrome car door handle from, I think, a Vauxhall Wyvern motor car which I had fashioned into a pirk. I tied this on to another rig with a small spoon and a large feathered hook. Once I was satisfied the hooks were secure – and in preparation for letting out line and starting pirking – I threw it overboard. It was then I realised I hadn't tied it to my main line! No more fish were caught on that outing.

Friday arrived at last and PK offered his services as ghillie. We drove down to Amhuinnsuidhe where the estate factor told us that we were to fish the Ladies Lochs – three small lochs situated immediately above a waterfall which flows into the sea. At high tide this waterfall is flooded and fish are seen jumping over it into a short stream which leads to the bottom and largest loch. It and the middle and top lochs are joined by short streams. Running into the top loch is a burn which flows down from more inland lochs.

There was a boat at the bottom loch and the three of us went out in it with PK on the oars. After a while I went ashore and fished from the bank. I soon hooked and landed a small salmon where the stream enters the bottom loch. I then moved up to the middle loch but didn't have an offer there. It was while I was there that I heard raised voices coming from the boat and when I ran down I saw Grigor with a fish on. It was jumping and splashing about and his nine foot rod was bent almost double.

I heard PK offering Grigor advice and I'll never forget his reply – "I know what I'm doing." Indeed, Grigor played the fish very competently and when the boat was brought in close to shore I netted a nice seven pounder. This was Grigor's first and last salmon on the fly, for he didn't inherit his father's passion for the game and seldom fished again. We continued fishing the three lochs until that evening. Although Grigor didn't catch any more, I landed a total of four salmon up to seven pounds and a three pound sea trout.

I took back all I had thought about Harris not being all that good for fishing. If you are in the right place at the right time it can be quite wonderful. Unfortunately, that was the last time I fished on Harris but I have many happy memories of that day. Incidentally, all the fish taken were on a size eight Butcher, fished on the tail.

Budding angler – my son Grigor at Altyre on the River Findhorn some years before landing his first salmon in Harris

15

Guns and rifles

If you have read this far into my scribblings, you will have realised that I am, without question, a right fishing nut. I am certainly not going to deny that, but angling has not been my only sporting passion. Over the years, I have been keen on shotgun and rifle shooting.

My shotgun experience was never that extensive and most of it was wildfowling in the Moray Firth. My memories of sitting in a muddy hole on the foreshore in freezing conditions, waiting for daylight and the slight possibility of a flight of ducks or geese happening to fly over my position, never really turned me on. I couldn't wait for the spring when the salmon season opened.

Rifle shooting, however, was a completely different story. I acquired a .22 with which I went on rabbit shooting expeditions, along with my sons Grigor and Paul when they were old enough. Many happy days we had, mainly in the Upper Findhorn valley where, before myxomytosis, rabbits were so plentiful that, when disturbed, the scattering rabbits made it appear as if the whole hillside was moving.

But it was deer stalking that really captured my interest. Through my days working in Grahams, before my National Service, I had made the acquaintance of many of the local gamekeepers – Jimmy Geddes, then Coignafearn; Duncan Davidson and Ian Watson, Glenmazeran; and Jock Stewart, Drynachan, to name but a few.

After joining the police, and while pounding the beat in Inverness, I met up with them again and expressed my interest in deer stalking. Duncan Davidson, who was then head keeper for Lord Elphinstone at Glenmazeran, invited me up to the estate to shoot my first hind. I was extremely excited at this prospect and the day was arranged. I did not, of course, have a deer rifle but Duncan assured me that one would be available for me to use.

It would have been in the late 1950s when I went on this first day's deer stalking with Duncan and under keeper Ian Watson, walking up the hills behind Glenmazeran Lodge as this was long before there were Argo-cats to help. I recall that we climbed to a wooded area called Cat Wood where Duncan, using a telescope, scanned the nearby hills.

On the opposite facing slope, directly across from Cat Wood, he spotted a number of hinds just above clumps of juniper bushes on the lower slopes of the valley between us. They were, of course, much too far away to shoot from where we lay, about four to five hundred yards. As a complete beginner, I had no idea how we could possibly get closer without exposing ourselves and frightening them away.

Duncan then explained that the three of us would walk in line with our heads bowed and hands behind our backs, and when he whispered 'walk' or 'stop' we would do as we were bid. I must say that I was completely mystified. We would be in complete view of the hinds for several hundred yards until we reached the cover of the juniper bushes at the bottom. Duncan walked in front, I was in the middle and Ian close behind, bringing up the rear. Duncan watched the hinds and, when he was satisfied that they had their heads down feeding, he would whisper 'walk'. When he saw them raise their heads to check out their vicinity, he would whisper 'stop'. I cannot remember how long it took us to walk/stop the distance between Cat Wood and the shelter of the junipers, but − much to my surprise − it did not spook the animals at all.

In many subsequent stalks – despite crawling as low to the ground as possible and taking advantage of every curvature of the ground and projecting foliage – I have been foiled frequently in attempts to get closer to my quarry. They ran off, probably laughing at this amateur stalker's pathetic attempts to put one over on them.

Having reached the junipers, we were now below our quarry. With Duncan still leading, we began to make our way slowly uphill through the bushes until, by standing on tip-toe looking over the top of the bushes, we could see the hinds. We moved further uphill until they were within range, but I could only see them if I stood with knees bent peering over the top of the junipers. It was impossible to find a spot where I could lie down to take up a normal prone shooting position and still see the beasts.

The rifle, a 6.5mm under lever action model which Duncan later told me had been used by the Queen Mother, was loaded by Ian and then handed to me. I was shaking with excitement and still wondering how on earth I was going to manage to make the shot. Then Duncan stood in front of me, slightly further uphill. Placing the rifle barrel over his right shoulder, he told me to take the shot. He stood, legs apart with his hands braced on top of his thighs. I braced myself behind him and, looking through the open sights, lined up on the particular hind that Duncan had selected for me to shoot.

After trying furiously to calm my jangling nerves, and when I was sure I had the beast solidly in the sights, I squeezed the trigger. Instead of the loud bang I anticipated, all that happened was a slight click. The rifle had misfired! To say the least, I was shattered. All that Duncan said was, "Aye, it does that sometimes."

I recocked the rifle and went through the whole palaver again. This time when I squeezed the trigger there was the expected loud bang and solid recoil against my shoulder. When I opened my eyes and looked the beast was down on the ground and the remaining members of its group were hightailing it up the hill and out of sight. When we approached the beast Duncan bled it and, with a bloodied finger, blooded me on my forehead. I had shot my first ever hind!

That was 50 years ago. Although Duncan and Ian are no longer with us and I have since shot countless hinds and many stags, I shall never ever forget that day. I suppose it is like landing your first salmon. It is a once in a lifetime experience and I have been lucky enough to have done both. I consider myself blessed.

15

Up the glen

Although I didn't really do a great deal of brown trout loch fishing in my early years in Inverness, I did do a fair bit of fishing on Loch Duntelchaig, one of the Inverness reservoirs. The fish from the crystal clear loch are few and far between but they are among the most beautifully marked I have ever seen, and the loch has some real beauties in it.

I used to cycle up to the loch and spin for trout, but also caught several pike up to 12 pounds there. A good day might yield about six fish with most being about the one pound mark. My biggest ever weighed 4½ pounds. My friend Bill Brown beat that with a 5½ pounder, but the best I heard of was a real thumper of 9¼ pounds which was taken by George MacKenzie who then worked for a motor spares company in Castle Street, Inverness. George later remustered as a ghillie on the Little Gruinard on the west coast of Scotland, ended his working days there and then returned to Inverness.

In the early 1970s, I met Iain MacCallum and his wife Maureen in town and, during our conversations, I learned that Iain worked for the Hydro Electric Board in Glenstrathfarrar, where they stayed at Deannie. They told me that directly in front of their house was Loch Beannacharan, further up the glen there was another loch, Mhuillidh, and right at the top of the glen was Loch Monar. I had heard of these waters and that they held good trout so when I was invited up to have a cast I quickly accepted. You had to get through a locked gate at the bottom of the glen and visiting the MacCallums was my key. I fished up there many times over the next few years and landed some very nice baskets

A basket of trout from Loch Mhuillidh

– all on the fly, I'm glad to say. There was always a cup of tea and a dram for me when I called on Iain and Maureen.

The River Farrar runs from a dam, with a fish pass, at the bottom end of Loch Beannacharan until it joins the River Glass at Struy and thereafter becomes the River Beauly. Salmon run up the Farrar and, after negotiating the dam on Loch Beannacharan, can move upstream, perhaps as far as below the Monar dam. In all the times I fished the lochs I had not sighted a salmon, until…

One afternoon I had fished around Loch Mhuillidh and was just in front of the old Hydro camp when I noticed, for the first time, the stream (it wasn't big enough to call a river) which runs out of the loch towards Loch Beannacharan. There was a nice deep pool a short way down from the loch and I thought it was worth a quick cast before I packed up for the day. I cast across the narrow stream and, much to my surprise, I saw a beautiful head and tail rise at my tail fly. The fish didn't connect with the fly but I was in no doubt that it was a salmon. I was tempted to cast over it once again, but thought that four pound breaking strain nylon was not the proper gear. I had a better idea. I drove back to the MacCallums and was so confident that I was going to catch this fish that I actually invited Iain and Maureen to witness it. Boy, was I right cocky! First I needed something. After a couple of scoops with a spade in their vegetable patch I got what I was looking for – three nice fat worms.

The three of us returned to the pool which, incidentally, Iain told me was beside long disused lead workings. I never knew there was lead in them thar hills! I put on a length of 10 pound breaking strain nylon, took out a hook, about size four, from my box and baited it up with the three worms, leaving long heads and tails to give plenty of movement, and dropped it into the neck of the pool. I hadn't moved more than five yards when I got the unmistakeable tug of a salmon mouthing the worms. I moved downstream to where I reckoned the fish would be and kept in touch with it by holding the line between thumb and forefinger. The knocking on the line continued for a short time and then the fish moved off towards the head of the pool. From my experience, that indicated that the fish was hooked and I tightened into it.

The fish jumped and ran around the small pool a couple of times before it tired and I drew it into the slack water where Iain picked it up and carried it away to safety. It was a reasonably fresh hen fish of about eight pounds. I would wager that very few salmon were ever caught so far up the system. It was the first time I could remember when I fished for and caught a specific fish, and said I would do so.

A year or two later I was fishing the far side of Loch Mhuillidh when, hand lining my flies alongside a patch of weed, I saw a fish break the surface as it took my fly. I got a quick look at it as it turned and, from the colour, I guessed it was a brownie, but a big one of at least six pounds. When I lifted the rod and tightened into it, the fish ran off alongside the weed bed towards the middle of the loch. I was very concerned that the fish would run into the weeds and entangle my line and hooks. Much to my surprise, however, every time it ran it skirted the weeds and stayed in clear water.

I had a particularly hard fight from this fish and when I eventually put my net under it and lifted it clear of the water, I was very surprised to see that it was a coloured cock salmon of seven pounds. The fly I took it on was a Heather Moth. I returned the fish, hopefully to join up later in the season with its all too few cousins who, like him, had managed to negotiate two fish passes on the River Beauly dams and one on the River Farrar at Loch Beannacharan in order to reach so far up the system – quite a journey, you will agree.

Further up the glen, after crossing the dam at Loch Monar, you can follow a rough track just about suitable for cars until you can go no further. After parking your vehicle there, you can follow a footpath up to the bottom of a huge hill to the left. There begins a climb as long and as steep as I've ever encountered. It is so steep that in one place it actually zigzags on itself. After about an hour you find yourself entering a hollow beneath Sgurr na Lapaich, from where a short walk over undulating terrain will reveal the reason for undertaking this long and arduous ascent. Lying beneath you are two lochans, known collectively as Tor Lochan. The smaller to the right is slightly higher than the other but both are just stuffed with small but very hard fighting trout.

In my young days, when I was fit, I made the effort to climb up to these lochans at least once a year. The fish were so plentiful there that I killed every one I caught. I firmly believe that there are so many trout there that killing all you catch gives the remaining fish better prospects of survival and the chance to grow bigger. Whether or not my theory was borne out, I do not know but on my last trip I actually caught a fish which weighed three quarters of a pound, a monster compared with the average weight of the normal bag.

The last time I climbed there would have been in the mid-1980s. On this occasion I was accompanied by my wife Anna and our faithful Labrador Ilé I. A work colleague Duncan 'Binns' MacKenzie, his wife Mairi and their two spaniels made up the rest of the party. On our arrival at the top loch Duncan and I set about pitching our tents, one of which I had borrowed from a friend. The women were a considerable distance behind us. All was going well until I realised I had forgotten to take the tent pegs. They were still in the boot of my car! To even consider returning to the car to collect them, and then repeat the climb, was out of the question. I borrowed a couple of pegs from Duncan which I placed at strategic positions to anchor the tent and the rest of it was held down by stones taken from the loch.

After a beautifully prepared meal we had taken with us, Duncan and I fished on until dark with the fish sometimes coming in three at a time. At about 11 pm I had had enough and returned to our tent along with Anna and Ilé, but Duncan continued for some time. Every fish he took he threw towards the tent. I fell asleep to the sound of these poor fish wriggling against the wall of our tent.

The following morning, very early, we got up and, leaving the tent, disturbed a group of deer grazing not far from our camp. The dogs enjoyed running after them until they were recalled. While the women cooked breakfast, the dogs joined Duncan and me on a walk up the hill towards the summit of Sgurr na Lapaich, a Munro at 3,775 feet.

We continued fishing until mid afternoon when we dismantled the tents, packed our bags and sorted out the catch which was in excess of one hundred trout. Those which were big enough for a frying pan were kept and the remainder thrown back into the lochan to feed the stock.

The walk back to the car was, in comparison to the climb, very easy and my bed at home was so much more comfortable than the heather mattress I had slept on the night before. But the view from my bedroom window could not compare with the view of Sgurr na Lapaich from our tent.

16

My 'MacNab'

The origins of this expression were immortalised in print by the author John Buchan who referred to an inveterate deer poacher of that name in his book. Today this refers to a sportsman who manages in one day to kill a stag, salmon and a brace of grouse, and has its history way back in the late 1800s.

In 1897, at a dinner being held in Inverness by the officers of the Militia Battalion of the Queen's Own Cameron Highlanders, one of the company, a Lt James Brander-Dunbar of Pitgaveney, near Elgin, announced that as he had not been invited to stalk anywhere that year, he would have to resort to poaching a beast. He laid a wager of £20 that he would kill a stag undetected on any deer forest in Scotland. A fellow officer, Captain James, 4th Lord Abinger, owner of Inverlochy Castle Estate, took up the challenge which he no doubt had to pay out on. And the rest, courtesy of John Buchan, is history.

Very few sportsmen have been able to achieve this glory, but I was able on two occasions in my sporting lifetime to score my own brand of a MacNab. The first time this happened was when my friend the late Dick Young had – courtesy of the late Captain Willie MacKay of Upper Glassburn, near Cannich – the shooting rights on the hills behind Glassburn House. Dick asked me one day in the late 1970s if I fancied having a shot at a stag and I jumped at the offer.

Early the next day we left Inverness and drove to Upper Glassburn, arriving there well before dawn. We climbed through the birchwoods which clothe the lower part of the slopes and, after a long breaktaking climb, reached the fence which separated the open hill from the woods. Daylight had just come in. After we climbed through the fence, which I recall was in a very poor state of repair, Dick led me up to a knoll which had an overall view of the fence for several hundred yards in each direction. We lay there and I loaded up my trusty .270 which I had used many times and with which I was confident.

After perhaps 20 minutes or so I saw a big stag, which had obviously spent the night grazing in the fields below, passing through a breach in the fence. It continued climbing on to the open hill and, once it went behind a hillock out of our sight, I followed Dick. We ran up behind the hillock and up to the crest. When we peered over the top I could see the beast, quite unconcernedly moving slowly up the hill with frequent stops to look back from where it had come.

"Will you manage it from here?" asked Dick, and I replied in the affirmative. The stag was about 80 to 100 yards away and at the same level as we were. Dick then said, "Neck shot?" I had already got myself into a shooting position and was looking at the stag through the telescopic sights of my rifle. I nodded and then, after taking a deep breath, squeezed the trigger. The beast collapsed, my shot hitting the exact point at which I had aimed.

There followed the gralloch which I had carried out many times. I was fortunate that this gory procedure didn't bother me, although I know many sportsmen who just cannot do it. Then began the drag back to the larder. One advantage of the ground was that it was all downhill and we were there almost before we knew it. The skinning didn't take us long and by almost 10 am we had finished and tidied the larder.

That same day Dick and his son Dennis had the tenancy of one of the beats on the River Conon and we drove over there. In those days the Conon was just stuffed with salmon and I had a wonderful day's sport, landing around 10 fish. The best weighed some 20 pounds, a very big one for the Conon.

My second experience was in September 1980 when I was fishing the Findhorn at Coignafearn, courtesy of my old pal Frank Stuart who was then the head keeper there. I had free run of the river at that time and, provided there was enough water, the salmon angling could be quite productive.

I was up the glen every day off then and one day Frank asked me if I fancied shooting a stag. I had shot many hinds there over the years but this was the first time I had been asked to shoot a stag. Frank explained that they were one stag short of their quota for that week and this was how the opportunity had arisen. Naturally, I agreed and the following day I arrived early in the morning with my .270, as well as my fishing rod.

Frank and I set off in the Argo, a six wheeled all terrain vehicle, and we headed for a part of the hill where Frank reckoned the River Findhorn is born. A spring rising there runs down to a burn which in turn joins another burn and eventually becomes the Findhorn, a good 12 to 15 miles upstream from Tomatin.

We exited the vehicle after spying the ground ahead of us and began a long slow crawl on all fours and on our bellies through sodden bogs and springy heather until Frank pointed out our quarry, a nice nine pointer. The only problem was there was a group of about half a dozen hinds between us and the stag which was a bit out of range at about 300 yards. Frank had earlier told me that he wanted any beast I shot to be neck shot and I wasn't confident enough to try it at that range. We waited for what seemed to be an eternity until the hinds moved off. We then crawled into a much closer position where I was able to complete the exercise in the manner hoped.

While I gralloched the stag, Frank went off for the Argo and on his return we loaded the stag into the vehicle and drove back to the larder. On our way there, on the river bank, we passed Bryan Allely who told us that he had had a wonderful day's sport, catching 10 salmon with his Allely Special fished on a trout fly rod.

After Frank and I finished skinning my stag and hanging it in the larder, I exchanged my rifle for my trout fly rod. Armed with a trout fly sized Black Shrimp, I began fishing opposite The Crofts and soon hooked and landed four grilse-sized fish.

These were my 'MacNabs'. But what about my brace of grouse to make up the tally, you ask? Oh, I forgot to tell you – I drank both of these!

17

Poaching

Apart from the Ericht salmon I witnessed being ripped or foul hooked when I was a boy, I had no further involvement with poaching until after I joined the Inverness Burgh Police. Even then this was not within my jurisdiction as it didn't take place within the burgh boundaries. In the surrounding County of Inverness, however, poaching of both salmon and deer was a common occurrence. Although these were attended to by my colleagues from Inverness County Police at their headquarters in Inverness Castle, sometimes I got involved in stopping cars to look for poached fish or game.

Following amalgamation, first with Inverness County and later with Ross and Cromarty and Caithness and Sutherland, I became more heavily involved with poaching when, for my sins, the Chief Constable appointed me Force Poaching Liaison Officer. A grand title, but this job – which included giving talks to police officers, water bailiffs and gamekeepers on the law as it related to poaching, and assisting in enquiries into local poaching cases – had to be carried on alongside my everyday duties as a Detective Sergeant in Inverness.

Telling evidence

One of the first salmon poaching cases I was actually involved in was when two men were reported acting suspiciously on the bank of the River Nairn near Daviot. They made off in their vehicle but were intercepted by a patrol car. The two men in the car were found to be soaking wet from the waist down and they had a fishing rod and reel loaded with very strong nylon line, but no terminal tackle. They admitted having been on the river bank but denied having done anything illegal.

A search of the river bank where they had been seen revealed a cache of seven salmon hidden under a bush. Lying nearby was a short length of nylon line, identical to the line on the reel, with a large treble hook and a lead weight attached to it. I examined the fish and found that each had tear marks on their left flanks (just like the Ericht salmon!) consistent with hook damage, and no marks whatsoever in their mouths.

The men were charged with poaching the salmon and pled not guilty. At their trial I gave evidence that in this particular pool where the men had been seen, on the north bank, fish faced upstream and the suspicious actions described by the witness were typical of the jerking rod action carried out by someone ripping or attempting to foul hook fish. The fact that all the fish had marks consistent with them having been foul hooked on their left flanks, the far side from the north bank, was evidence that they had been foul hooked by someone standing on the north bank of the river. The absence of any marks in their mouths refuted the possibility that they had been legally hooked. They were both convicted and received substantial fines.

The graveyard shift

Another incident, also involving the River Nairn, took place in Nairn itself. Complaints had been made that locals, in broad daylight, were ripping salmon from the River Nairn just above the main A96 road bridge. A police presence there during daylight hours put a stop to that, but the practice apparently continued after dark.

It was decided that after darkness fell a cordon of police, water bailiffs and committee members of Nairn Angling Club would surround the area and, by using radios, the watchers would be notified by a constable strategically placed close to the pool when he was satisfied that a fish had been taken. Then the other cordon members would close in and, hopefully, make an arrest.

This particular night, along with a water bailiff, I hid in undergrowth on the east side of the river and waited for something to happen. We hadn't been there long when I heard splashing and swishing noises coming from the pool about 250 yards away. The swishing noises obviously came from the fishing rods being jerked violently. Not long afterwards I heard the unmistakeable sound of a fish splashing in shallow water and, a few seconds later, the thump, thump sound of it being killed by blows to the head. But where was the radio message to close in? It never came and I later learned that the bobby who was to raise the alarm had a faulty radio and didn't know what to do.

Meantime, I could hear the sound of someone fording the river and imagined that this would be the poacher making off with the fish. He was, however, moving away from me in the direction of the graveyard where I knew my colleague Aeneas MacKay was stationed and he would grab him.

Later, Aeneas told me that from his position in the graveyard he couldn't see the river. But he could hear noises which suggested something was going on down there. Like the rest of us, he wondered why there was no radio message asking us all to close in. Then all had gone quiet and, shortly afterwards, he heard footsteps coming in his direction from the river. He thought it was me coming up to tell him that we had either caught someone or the operation was off. He then saw a figure approaching and, in the half dark, could clearly see the silver flash of a salmon which this man was holding. He realised it was a poacher.

Aeneas lay down alongside a flat gravestone and, as the person was just in front of him, he stood up and said, "Got ya," or some similar phrase which policemen use in such circumstances. The poacher, obviously thinking that it was a spirit of the dead rising up to claim him for his sins, let out a scream which was so loud I heard it on the other side of the river, dropped the fish and ran off yelling at the top of his voice, never to be seen again.

I'll bet he never went poaching in the dark again! The fish was given to an old folks home.

Fateful recognition

As part of my duties as Poaching Liaison Officer I was instructed to travel to the Western Isles to make discreet enquiries regarding the salmon poaching problem there. The situation there was getting a bit out of hand with commercial style methods and violence – for example, attempting to ram bailiffs' boats with sea going vessels – becoming too prevalent. It was early in July when I travelled to Lewis and only Chief Inspector D A Morrison on the island was aware of the reason for my visit. My cover was that I was on a fishing holiday and I took bed and breakfast with a Mrs MacArthur in Carloway. This was pretty central to the area in which I was to make my enquiries.

I did go fishing for brown trout on several local lochs and didn't catch much, but I called on the gamekeepers on most of the estates in the area which had poaching problems and discussed the matter with them. During my enquiries I learned that a remote pub in this area would be worth a look as poaching activities were believed to stem from there.

I will never forget that day. I fished this particular loch which entailed a very long walk in and back out. It rained almost all day and I was drookit and in need of a warming beverage. A double whisky sounded about right so I decided that it would be an ideal time to visit this particular hostelry. It was shortly after five pm when I entered the bar, still wearing my thigh boots and shaking my soaking wet jacket. I saw a barmaid, a young woman in her mid twenties, behind the bar and there were three customers. The first gentleman was sitting in a corner alone and the other two were standing at the bar.

I ordered a large whisky and stood at the bar between the two men and the one in the corner. I attempted to make conversation but it was rather difficult as the others were all speaking Gaelic. I imagined that I was probably the topic of their conversation. "Who is this man coming in here all wet and looking lost?"

I finished my dram and decided that there didn't appear to be any point in remaining there. Then the old man in the corner said to the barmaid, "You'd better give the gentleman a dram." I accepted the dram and began talking to the man about how dour I had found the trout on the loch I had fished. Then I thought I would cement the relationship by buying a round of drinks for everyone there. I offered them all a drink and, when handing over a £10 note, asked the barmaid to have one herself. She served the drinks and, when handing me the change, she cocked her head to one side and said, "It's John Cathcart, isn't it? Are you still in the police?"

I don't think I have ever been so shocked. I couldn't imagine being in such a remote part of the world and still being recognised! I spluttered "Yes" and asked how she knew me. She told me that she used to work in a hotel in Inverness and remembered me coming in there to sell salmon.

As if that wasn't bad enough, right on cue the door of the bar opened and two men wearing sou'westers, oilskin jackets and waders came in and I heard them mention nets as they approached the bar. The poor old man in the corner just about fell off his stool trying to catch these men's attention and began to speak to them in Gaelic. This is a language I know very little about but I did recognise the word 'polis'. The atmosphere in the bar became very strained then so I just finished my drink and bid them all cheerio before going out into the rain. I didn't return to that pub during my visit!

The salmon and the flat fish

I was aware that, in an attempt to stop the ever-worsening salmon poaching in Loch Roag, the Grimersta Estate had arranged for a large seagoing vessel to be stationed on the loch to assist the bailiffs in their anti-poaching patrols. I was present when this boat, the Omsk, sailed in and anchored at the head of the loch and I was invited to go out in the boat that afternoon while the skipper charted the channel so that he could come in, even at low water. Two small boats, one an inflatable and each with a bailiff on board, set off ahead of us to check the north and south shorelines for any illegal nets which may have been set there.

Not long after we set out there was a radio call from the bailiff on the inflatable, then out of sight ahead of us on the south side of the loch, to the effect that he had found a poacher. The other bailiff shot across the loch to join him.

When we rounded the headland a short time later, I saw a man standing upright at the back of his wooden rowing boat and holding on to the throttle of his outboard motor, which was going flat out. The inflatable was zigzagging in front of him in an attempt to slow him down and the other bailiff was travelling alongside the poacher. Suddenly, the poacher veered sharply to one side and, intentionally or by accident, he rammed the inflatable amidships and it ended up draped across the bows of the poacher's boat. Both came to a sudden halt and how neither man was pitched into the water I will never know.

I decided that it was about time I became involved and asked for the other bailiff to return to the Omsk and pick me up, which he quickly did. By the time I got over to the other two boats the bailiff and poacher were both ashore and arguing fiercely. I produced my warrant card and identified myself to the poacher. I learned from the bailiff that he came across the man attempting to pull a set net out of the water. After the bailiff had identified himself, the man continued to pull his net from the water. When the bailiff caught hold of the net the poacher attempted to cut the net with a knife.

At this point I informed the man that he was under arrest for poaching, but he took to his heels up the hill towards a nearby house. I ran after him and on our arrival at the house, where I saw a net draped over the garden fence, we were met by a man who I assumed was the poacher's father. He asked me what was going on. I identified myself to him and informed him that his son was under arrest for poaching. The poacher then insisted he had only been fishing for flat fish. When I asked if he had a telephone I could use, they told me they didn't have one. On an earlier recce of the area, I had noted a nearby public telephone from which I called the police at Stornoway and asked Chief Inspector Morrison to arrange for a uniformed officer to call at the poacher's house as soon as possible. On returning to the house I really felt out of it again as all the conversation was in Gaelic.

Half an hour later the constable from Carloway arrived and my poacher was arrested and taken to Stornoway to spend the night there. Back at the shore, I examined the boat and net. I found silvery scales in the boat and took some of them as I suspected they were salmon scales. I also took possession of the net and boat. In light of the poacher's defence that he had been fishing for flat fish, I asked that the depth at which the net had been fished be measured and also the depth of water in which it had been set be checked at low water. If the net touched the bottom, there was substance to his defence.

On the way back up to the head of the loch, with the poacher's boat in tow, the boat's radio was almost red hot with transmissions from crofters and the like whose homes overlooked Loch Roag, saying for example, "Donald has been caught lock, stock and barrel with his net by bailiffs from that big boat which arrived yesterday," "Aye, that will be them from that Grimersta Estate," and "Aye, there will be trouble tonight at the head of the loch."

In view of all this I told the skipper to ensure that he left someone on board the Omsk that night, as I feared that some form of reprisal might be planned. I was right. At three o'clock the following morning a frogman was caught climbing aboard. His excuse was that he was only climbing aboard out of curiosity to see what the boat was like. But I'll bet that if he hadn't been caught the Omsk would have been found lying on the bottom the next day!

Incidentally, the frogman – a 'white settler' – later appeared at Stornoway Sheriff Court and was fined for a breach of the peace. If his intended mission had been accomplished, I'm sure that many a dram would have been put up the bar for him by locals!

The scales I took were identified as salmon and the depth of water where the net had been set was found to be deeper than the depth of the net, even at low water. The poacher pled not guilty and I had to appear to give my evidence against him. After all the prosecution witnesses had given their evidence, the accused cited a friend who stated that he had known flat fish to have been caught where the net had been set. The accused himself then opted to give evidence on his own behalf. That day I witnessed a unique courtroom exchange. The Sheriff, the late Scott-Robinson, asked the poacher several questions:

Q	"Who uses this boat besides yourself?"
A	*"Family."*
Q	"What members of your family?"
A	*"Just family."*
Q	"What do you use the boat for?"
A	*"Fishing."*
Q	"What kind of fishing?"
A	*"For mackerel and flat fish."*
Q	"When do you use the boat?"
A	*"In the summer."*
Q	"When do you mean, in the summer?"
A	*"July and August."*
Q	"When do the salmon begin running in Loch Roag?"
A	*"July."*

My poacher was found guilty and given a nominal fine. His boat was not confiscated.

Devastation by the dark side

Unquestionably the darkest side of poaching is when the perpetrator resorts to using poison to kill the fish. I have twice seen the after effects of some idiots, who obviously didn't care a hoot for the consequences, tipping probably a whole tin of Cymag or other similar oxygen depleting substance into a river. These poachers would take as many salmon as they could carry away from the pool, leaving the deadly effects of their actions to carry on downstream for many miles killing all fish, insects and other oxygen-dependant life until it became sufficiently diluted to no longer pose a threat to life. The stretch of river from the point where the poison was introduced to the lower point was reduced to a barren waste and would take many months, probably years, to recover to its previous state.

The first occasion I encountered this was shortly before I retired from the police in 1985. I was called to the River Nairn, upstream of Daviot, where a passer-by had reported seeing a number of dead salmon floating in the water. It was during August and there was a good stock of fish in the river. On looking into the river, which is quite shallow at that point, I saw a dead grilse lying on its side and a number of parr and a small brown trout, also dead.

It appeared that the river had been poisoned above this point so I walked about 200 yards upstream to a deep pool. After watching for about 20 minutes, I saw a couple of grilse jumping quite naturally at the neck of the pool. On the beach at the middle and tail of the pool, and below the waterline, there were recent footprints in the sand. These were all indistinct and of no value for taking plaster casts. To me it appeared that this is where the criminal, or criminals, had put in the poison and possibly netted the fish. I walked downstream for over two miles and saw dead fish in most of the pools down to that point. Clearly, too much poison had been put into the water. Helped by a local resident, I removed over 60 fish from the river. The fry and trout were just left.

The nearest I got to solving this was when I learned that a local fishmonger had received a telephone call from a man offering to sell him "large sea trout." He didn't phone back but I am sure that the large sea trout would have been small grilse of four to six pounds which is typical of the main summer stock.

The second occasion was in July 1995 when a local solicitor who had connections with a proprietor of the River Carron in Ross-shire asked me to investigate a suspected case of poisoning in the river.

When I arrived at this beautiful river, just below Glencalvie Falls, I was met by a sight I never wish to see again. Gamekeepers were

Devastating – just some of the fish killed by poison on the River Carron

driving tracked vehicles pulling bogeys which were spilling their loads of dead salmon! These had all been removed from the pools immediately below the falls. Some 1,200 salmon and grilse were removed and buried but we'll never know just how many more were not recovered. The cause of their deaths was oxygen deprivation – poisoning. Written in chalk on a rock at the side of the falls was the word 'THINK'.

I learned from police and local gamekeepers that they strongly suspected a local, with some grudge against the estate, as the perpetrator of this heinous crime. Unfortunately, there was insufficient evidence to make a case against him. I know a lot of people who would like to have a quiet word with him – just to show him the error of his ways, of course!

On The Beat

18

Days to remember

The number of fish caught in a day does not necessarily make the day noteworthy but I do recall fishing on the River Moriston in the opening week of the 1974 season. It was one of the best opening weeks on record and I was lucky enough to have been there.

On the opening day, Glen Quoich keeper George Stoddard took two fish weighing 14 and 16 pounds, and the resident keeper Jimmy MacDonnell took an 18 pounder.

The next day Inverness angler Bill Godsman had a nice 10 pounder, but Jimmy MacDonnell put that in the shade when he landed his heaviest ever weighing 26 pounds. I was on hand to help him land it. On the same day, using large Rapala lures, I called on Jimmy's services to help me land two weighing 18½ and 19 pounds. Another angler landed a 25 pounder the same day and, at the end of that week, Inverness angler Graham MacKenzie finished what was one of the finest opening weeks ever with a 14 pounder.

I had many more trips to the Moriston in the spring months and, although I caught several more fish, I will never forget the brace I took that year. Unfortunately, I was not on the Moriston the following week as the bonanza continued and I think it is worth telling again.

On the Monday Jimmy MacDonnell had, for him, a small one at 10 pounds and Mr Forbes had one of the same weight. On the Tuesday under keeper Ken Brown showed us that all the big ones

130

hadn't gone when he took a thumper of 24 pounds and Jimmy Johnson had one of 10 pounds.

Wednesday was a record-breaking day when Alan Scott landed what was found to be the largest fish from the river since records began, weighing in at 34 pounds. It was hooked on a three-treble Rapala lure and was landed within five minutes. What an anti-climax! Alan, after seeing the fish just below the surface, expected to have to fight it for about an hour at least but, obviously, was happy to have it safe on the bank. The apparent explanation for its lack of fight was that the hooks on the lure were all fixed into

Those were the days – Alan Scott with his 34 pound springer from the River Moriston

The biggest salmon the author has ever seen – a 38 pounder taken from Loch Ness by Torry MacKenzie

the top and bottom jaws and, being unable to breathe, it soon gave up the fight.

This big fish wasn't alone as Jimmy MacDonnell proved when his next fish, weighing 23 pounds, was landed and the day was rounded off when Jimmy Johnson took his second of the week, a 12½ pounder. On the Thursday, big fish were still about and Ken Brown and H MacDonald each landed fish weighing 20 and 16 pounds respectively. Jimmy McDonnell was the only rod in action on the Friday when he caught another thumper of 20 pounds. On Saturday, Fort William angler A MacGillvray finished off the week with one of 24 pounds.

Incidentally, the scale reading of Alan's 34 pounder showed that it was five years old, having spent two years in fresh water before migrating to the sea in the spring of 1971 as a six inch smolt and coming back three years later measuring 44 inches in length, 27 inches in girth and weighing 34 pounds. That's what you call having the right diet!

Only recently I learned that the River Moriston was, in the past, renowned for its big brown trout. It was only in Victorian times,

Another massive fish – Alex MacDonald of the Fort Augustus Tackle Shop with a magnificently shaped 34 pound River Oich fish

when the falls on the lower stretch of the river were blasted to allow salmon access to the spawning areas in the river's upper reaches, that it developed into one of the finest spring rivers in the country.

Another day I will never forget is the first day I ever fished on the River Conon, on this occasion on the Coull Beat. It was not long after I had left the RAF and my old friend Bill Brown was with me. I recall using my recently acquired Playfair spliced greenheart rod, 14 feet in length, for about the first time. Bill and I landed four apiece and lost several. They were all in the six to eight pound class, but fought like lions. The flies I caught them

Best of memories – with Bill Brown (left) and part of our catch from the Coull Beat of the River Conon

on were, from memory, home made efforts with yellow hair wings – Garry Dog variants I suppose. This was the first day I had ever managed to land more than one salmon on the fly in a day. For that reason it remains one of my best memories.

The Spey was the scene of another of my big catch days. On this occasion I was fishing with pals Bryan Allely, Alec and Charlie MacDonald, and Rae Woods and his nephew of the same name. We were fishing Brae Water Beats One and Two. Our ghillies were John White and the late George Sutherland, known as Bunter, and we certainly kept them busy with a total bag of 37 fish. Spinning was permitted in those days and I have to admit that the bulk of the catch was taken by that method. The lure that did most of the damage that day – and continued to do so on many, many days over the years since, including the 2006 season – was my two inch Aswood devon in its dark red livery. Incidentally, my share of the bag was 12 fish.

Another memorable day on the Spey was when Bryan, Alec, Charlie, Rae and I gathered outside the hut on Castle Beat Number One below the road bridge at Fochabers to begin our three days there. It was in September and the river was very high. The ghillie told us there was a good head of fish in the river with a good number of clean run fish among them.

I was allocated the tail end of the Slabs Pool which is a very broad pool necessitating deep wading. I was fishing my 17 foot Diawa rod, a full sinking line and a large number two Red Prawn fly which I found to be particularly useful in the back end. I had one of my best ever days fly fishing, landing 10 salmon of which the best weighed 27 pounds.

Before I finish this chapter I must mention the upper reaches of the River Findhorn, particularly around Tomatin where, depending on water levels and temperature, the fish usually arrived in numbers about the end of May. I have known them to arrive that far upstream as early as late April but only in ones and twos. In the good old days, the 1970s, late May into early June was the time to be there.

A perfect example of how good it used to be was the year 1978. In mid May reports were received that the fish were over the falls on the lower Findhorn (it is known that salmon will not go over these falls until the water temperature rises to 42 degrees Fahrenheit) and expectations were high for their imminent arrival at Tomatin. The first to score there was local angler Jock MacLeod who landed three weighing between eight and 12 pounds on Tomatin House water, and his son John took a fourth.

The fish were soon in every beat, even as far upstream as Coignafearn where Olive Stewart, wife of head keeper Frank, hooked a nice fish. Just as she was about to land it the family terrier Shane, who had been watching the play with some interest, decided it was time he took part in the proceedings and jumped straight into the water on top of the fish. This was just

My brother-in-law Mick Stone with a Findhorn salmon taken at Coignafearn

too much for Olive's tackle and the line snapped! Shane was immediately returned home in disgrace but happily, within a few casts, another salmon was hooked. This time all went well and a nice clean run nine pounder was landed.

Downstream at Glenmazeran five was their best day's score with the heaviest weighing 17 pounds. Back down on the Tomatin House stretch the MacLeod duo took another seven fish and Bryan Allely and I had a particularly good day with seven between us, weighing from seven to 12 pounds. But the best individual catches were made on the Balnespick beat by the keeper there, the late Jimmy Geddes. He took seven salmon with the heaviest weighing 16, 17, 18 and 30 pounds. This monster was a typical Findhorn fish, thin by Ness fish standards. It measured 45 inches in length.

Jimmy Geddes displays his 30 pound Findhorn salmon

19

One Offs

Sometimes things happen to us when our companions either do or say something which fits in with the incident, making it more humorous.

One such incident happened to me during the 2005 season. A particularly bad run of luck on the Inverness Angling Club waters had seen me lose no fewer than eight salmon consecutively. No matter what I did, the fish − all hooked spinning which, unfortunately, is the only method I can now do − all fell off the hook before they could be brought within range of a net.

I walked up to the Weir Pool from the Mill Stream and, after chatting with the boys sitting on the bench at the bottom, went up to the top of the pool. I had fished down to a point opposite the seat, where the boys were still enjoying their coffee and a blether, when bang! − I was into one.

The fish was a beauty of about 16 pounds and, much to my relief, it didn't run out of the pool down towards the Mill Stream, as did most of the fish I had hooked there. I soon had it almost ready for netting and was joined at the water's edge by 'Action Man', the late lamented Raymond Black, armed with a big net.

I began to draw the fish, which was pretty well done in, towards Raymond's net. When the fish was literally inches from the net, there was a cry from the bench, "Come in number nine, your time's up." At that precise moment, the hooks fell out of the fish's mouth and it floated away! I must say I wasn't too happy, but what can you say at a moment like that. I'm just waiting and hoping that I can return the favour one day to Kevin 'Keevo' MacDonald.

On another occasion I was fly fishing on the Findhorn and, with the aid of my walking stick, had positioned myself at the top of a run where I could cover the water. I felt the pull and was into a fish, a clean run grilse of about five pounds.

I could not move as I needed the stick and rod butt to help me, so I shouted to my friend who was fishing about one hundred yards downstream. He came running up and I quickly brought the fish into the shallow water where he picked it up by the tail and behind the head. He then began to walk up the steep gravel bank away from the water.

About half way up he turned to face me, holding the fish out in front of him, and said, "John, it really is a beauty." The fish then wriggled and he dropped it and shouted, "Tighten the line!" I could see that the fish was no longer hooked and, in a flash, it had wriggled across the gravel, back into the water and was gone.

My friend was profuse in his apologies but there was nothing he could do, so I said, "Just forget it…" I don't want to name and embarrass him now.

On our next visit to the same Findhorn beat I was fishing upstream of my friend when he got into a fish. I hobbled down to give him a hand to land it, positioned myself in the shallow water and waited for him to bring the fish to me. When the fish, a slightly coloured hen of about nine pounds, swam within reach I grabbed it firmly by the tail and lifted it up.

I just couldn't resist stopping on the way inshore and saying. "…, it really is a beauty." However, I didn't drop it until I was well away from the water. The look on his face when I stopped was better than any apology!

20

Ones that got away

In everyone's fishing experiences there have been days when we have hooked a fish which we have believed was our fish of a lifetime and, as luck would have it, we lost the blooming thing!

Many times we guess the size of these fish by either the length of time it was on the line or by the sheer strength of it. But the only sure way to be close to the truth is to actually see it. This observation is very often far from accurate as the angler is most open to exaggeration, especially if it is his own fish.

In my lifetime I have hooked several salmon which I just could not control, both on the fly and spinning, and wondered if this could be the one. But these fish never broke surface and I only know that they were big! Unfortunately, they all came off and I wonder to this day if that one I hooked on the MacIntyre Pool of the Ness, the one I lost in the Spey or the one which broke my 23 pound fly cast in the Canadian Kitimat river were record breakers.

Of course, they might all have been foul hooked. That would account for their extraordinary strength. We have all, at one time or another, foul hooked salmon and know that even a five pounder, hooked by the tail, can feel like a 20 pounder for a while. I think back, however, to four salmon I hooked, saw and didn't kill which, without boasting, I can say were even heavier than my 32½ pound Tay fish.

Mistaken identity

The first of these was while I was fishing the Netting Water Pool on the Dochfour Beat of the Ness. It was during May in the late

1950s and I was spinning with the first wooden devon I had ever bought, a 3½ inch brown and gold, when I hooked the fish.

I don't know how long I played it, but it would have been in excess of an hour before I got it into a convenient backwater where I managed to bring it ashore. I recall that it was a cock fish, fat as a barrel and almost half the length of my spinning rod. There was only one thing wrong. The fish was coloured – not like a back-end fish but purpley coloured with the silver still shining through.

I was very inexperienced then and, after a great deal of deliberation, I gave the fish the benefit of my misgivings and put it back into the river where it swam off, apparently none the worse of its experience. I thought then that I had caught a very well mended kelt or perhaps a baggot – a fish which had not gone through the reproductive process.

Afterwards, however, having given it a great deal more thought, I realised that by May all kelts, particularly late downstream runners, would have turned from their spawning colours back to silver in preparation for their return to the sea. I had put back a perfectly good early run springer whose original bright silver colouring had been tarnished after perhaps two or three months in fresh water. I estimated that it would have weighed not less than 35 pounds!

A light line regret

My second possible record fish was hooked on the Laggan Pool of the Ness one June in the early 1960s. That forenoon I had fished with my work colleague, Willie Armstrong Snr. Although we didn't catch anything, I did see a grilse rise – the first I had seen that season. We both had to return to work for a short time that day and I asked Willie if he was going to fish again that afternoon. He said that he had better attend to some work in his garden.

I then had a thought. As the river was on the low side any running fish would be inclined to slow down and perhaps lie for a while in the neck of the pool and that the worm might be worth a try there. I dug up part of my garden and gathered half a jar of earth worms and thought that, as I would be fishing for grilse, a light line of seven pounds breaking strain would give me the ability to cover the breadth of the pool with ease. It was a big mistake!

Returning to the Laggan, I began casting the worm with a couple of split shot on the line and soon encountered some nibbles, obviously from small trout. I discouraged these and kept moving slowly down the pool. I then stuck fast on the bottom and, after pulling hard and expecting to break the line, it came free. I did not retie my knots – big mistake number two! – but put on another worm and cast again. I was fishing with the spinning reel bale arm open, the line held lightly between my thumb and forefinger and slowly walking downstream keeping in line with the bait. Then, without any noticeable tug on the line, it began to move upstream. I let the line go and watched it peel off the spool until I realised that more than 20 yards had been taken. I then had no doubt that a salmon had taken the bait while moving up the pool and that it had continued up the pool without halting. This was my first and last experience of this kind.

Realising that the fish must have the hook well in its mouth, I dropped my forefinger to catch the line and closed the bale arm as I raised the rod to strike. Immediately I felt the weight of the fish and saw a huge silver shape partly hidden in the spray which was atomised by the very strong breeze. The fish took off across the breadth of the pool which is about 100 yards wide at this point. I had no option but to let the fish go as I realised that I couldn't possibly dictate to it with my light tackle. Then a wonderful thing happened! The fish, which had obviously been running hard, probably since it had left salt water, turned on its side exhausted. It was as if someone was holding a huge mirror, turning it under the water and flashing it towards me in the bright sunlight.

I managed to bring the fish back across to my side of the river without any trouble at all. It was fairly deep water where I was standing, and not ideal for trying to gaff a fish. Knowing the layout of the pool, I decided to gently lead the fish downstream until I could wade out in the shallower water until I was in line with the fish and then gaff it. It was offering no resistance at all.

All went well. I positioned myself directly in line below the fish when, for no reason at all as I didn't have any strain on it, the line just parted. I was distraught but thought the gods were still with me for the fish, still on its side, continued to float down towards me. I still had a chance. I waited and waited as the fish floated nearer and nearer the gaff.

Then I did something which I will regret for the rest of my life. Just as the fish was inches out of range of my gaff, I moved my feet to position myself for the final act. This movement wakened up the salmon which immediately turned upright and, with a flick of its tail, disappeared. Fortunately, there was no-one within earshot to hear my outburst or to see the tears in my eyes as I waded ashore. Oh to have had someone with me, or if I hadn't moved too soon! It could have been so different.

I got a really good look at that fish and reckon that it would have turned the scales at around 35 pounds. I have relived that experience many times over in the ensuing decades.

A tale from the tail

My third nearly record fish story was when, during 1972 or thereby, I was fishing the Dochfour beat in August. I was alone on the Lower Beat while ghillie Bill Paton was on Beat One with a guest.

I had crossed over to the island at the top of the main pool and fished down to a very good lie known as Tail of the Island when my fly was taken by a fish which, unlike the bulk of the salmon I was hooking then, did not immediately come to the surface and splash about like a sea trout. This one kept down and, initially, all that happened was it just shook its head. This went on for quite a while and then it seemed to wake up. It shot downstream ripping line off my reel and soon the splice between my casting line and backing was right out of sight.

I made my way downstream as fast as I could, retrieving line as I went, but as soon as I got opposite the fish, which still hadn't broken the surface, it ran back up to where I had hooked it. This suited me as the fish now also had to fight the current. I remained below the fish for, I guess, a full half an hour, with me laying into it and it forging further and further upstream. Then, what I hoped would happen, the fish began to drop down, obviously becoming exhausted but maintaining its position in the middle of the river.

Knowing that there were some very large stones in the pool which could become hazards, I left the water and climbed up on to the path about 10 feet above the river. I continued to play the fish and my intention was to bring it down to the bottom third of the pool to an even gravel beach which I thought would be ideal for beaching it.

I then got my first look at the fish. I knew that it had to be a very good one, maybe a 20 pounder, but when I saw it just below the surface I realised that this was something in a different league. I had been playing it for well over an hour and my arms were aching. But the fish was gradually coming nearer and nearer my bank and every time I saw it I was becoming more and more excited, for this could be my fish of a lifetime.

All my attention was being directed at my fish and I didn't see or hear this person walking up towards me until he spoke. "Hello John, can I give you a hand?" It was young Dennis Young. I really thought that the gods were with me. Dennis was wearing thigh boots so I gave him my gaff and asked him to wade out a bit and I would try to bring the fish to him. He waded out until he was in just above his knees and I told him to remain there. I began backing up, bringing the fish closer and closer to Dennis. But it almost seemed to know and just would not come in that extra two or three feet.

I have a lasting picture in my mind. Dennis – who, like his dad is a six-footer – is leaning forward with the gaff raised. Upstream of him I can see the head of the fish. Downstream of him I can see its tail. That is when the hook falls out and the fish just floats away out of reach until it flicks its tail and disappears.

How big was it? Certainly well into the 30 pounds, in my estimation. When recalling the story recently with Dennis, he said he had seen many 30 pounders and he guesses that mine must have been 40! He will never forget the fright he got when he first saw it. Never before or since had he seen one so big.

End of a roll

The fourth of my nearly record fish stories was while I was fishing at the bottom of the Cumberland Pool on the Lower Castle Waters of the Spey, below Fochabers, around 1990. I had had a very successful day, landing five or six fish of up to 18 pounds. The day before I had caught 10 with the best weighing 27 pounds. I was on a roll!

I was fishing with my 17 foot Diawa rod, a number 11 sinking line and a size two treble prawn-type fly. I was wading quite deep across a point where the river broke to my left to form an island and, if I left my cast to fish too long, it was drawn over into the side stream. I normally cast again before this point was reached.

On this particular cast the line had swung round until it was almost directly below me and, as I was preparing to cast, the line stopped dead. I immediately lifted my rod but there was no movement and I thought that I had caught on the bottom. I gave it a couple of hard pulls. Nothing happened so I shortened line and pulled again. Still nothing. Then, fully 40 seconds after I had first struck, the line started to move slowly upstream.

I hand lined to keep the line tight until the fish – clearly that's what it was – moved opposite and then upstream of my position. I was then obliged to let out some of the slack line I had gathered. By this time I was becoming quite excited. What manner of fish was this? It certainly wasn't a foul hooked fish for they invariably move off very quickly once the hook touches them. Bryan Allely was fishing below me and he asked if I was stuck on the bottom. I replied, "No, it's a fish, but I don't know what's going on."

With that the fish accelerated and, no more than 15 yards in front of me, this huge beast leaped out of the water. It was only there for a split second but in that time I clearly saw that it was a cock fish with a very well developed kype. It was slightly coloured and I could see my fly hanging from the side of its mouth. After it returned to the river, all the remaining slack line I had was ripped through the rod rings and the reel began to scream. Then disaster, everything went slack. The fish was off. On winding in, I found that the hook was in perfect order.

What I think happened was that the fish had taken my fly at depth without moving much, if at all. Consequently, I felt no pull as it took. I was unlucky as the large kype left space at the side of the fish's mouth which allowed the fly to escape without hooking it properly. What size did I think it was? Bearing in mind that I had caught a 27 pounder the previous day and was fairly familiar with big fish, I would honestly guess that this brute would have been close to 40 pounds. OK, we accept that anglers are inclined to exaggerate so I'm prepared to knock off two pounds from my estimate of the weights of these FOUR fish, the biggest I have hooked, seen and lost!

2/

Tackle making

Ever since I fashioned my first hook out of a bent pin, I have had a penchant for making fishing tackle which developed, slowly, over the years. I began by tying trout and salmon flies without the aid of a vice. My first salmon on a fly I had tied myself, with a clump of my own hair (I called it Curly – I wonder why?) was caught on the River Nairn. I thought, "Who needs Blue Charms any more?" But I realised that my thick curly hair was not best suited for wing material and changed to using squirrel tail.

The next venture into tackle making, during the time I was working in Grahams, was to make spoons out of flattened copper from old plumbing pipes. A very successful but very expensive spoon was, I recall, the Hardy Greenwell. This lure was unique in that it was finished in a dull, non-reflective coat that was apparently deadly for salmon. The cost of these was prohibitive but Bill Brown and I reckoned we could make reasonable copies, which we did. With these spoons I accounted for very many kelts, a number of salmon and some pike in the years before my National Service. I haven't heard of the Greenwell spoon since then, over 50 years ago. I wonder if there are still any around now?

A leader in lead

Moving on to the late 1950s, by which time I was in the police, the only lure to use on the Ness or on the sea trout fishings at Clachnaharry or North Kessock was a Jock Dyce minnow. Jock, who was then working as a stevedore at the harbour, was one of the finest anglers on the river and on the foreshore. He was also one of the finest makers of lead minnows I ever met.

From a length of lead electric cable cover he could – in a few minutes and with a few taps of a hammer – fashion a beautifully balanced devon into which he glued Perspex fins. A coat of silver paint and it was ready to go. Of the sea trout taken from the foreshore in those days, when they were plentiful, I reckon Jock's minnows would have accounted for fully half of them.

Many anglers, including myself, made their own variations of this type of lure and they were responsible for catching many more salmon. The one problem with them was that they were really too heavy for shallow river fishing and many ended up lying on the bed of the river, never to be seen again.

The wooden devon

Then someone in the Aberdeenshire area invented the weighted wooden devon, although I understand that unweighted wooden devons had been in use in such rivers as the Wye long before this. But the new variant had a copper tube through the body, giving it a near perfect weight for casting and fishing in shallowish waters such as the Ness. I was among the first to buy one of these and it was on this lure that I hooked probably one of my largest salmon ever (see Ones that got away).

My late buddy Steve Fraser and I met up in the early 1960s and it wasn't long before we put our heads together and decided that we could make wooden devons as good as the ones on sale in the shops. Searching through catalogues, we eventually found a small lathe suitable for turning wooden blanks up to four inches in length. We set it up in Steve's garage and I went to the local scrap yards where I bought old copper brake piping. Steve went to his joiner friend for one inch by one inch lengths of various types of wood to experiment with until we found the most suitable for the purpose. Oak was too hard, pitch pine was too soft but beech seemed to be what we were after.

The copper pipe was cleaned, straightened and then cut into lengths slightly longer than the size of the lure we intended to make. The wood was also cut into lengths longer than the intended length of the lure. Then came the tricky bit. We had to drill the block of wood lengthwise with a bit that was a slightly smaller gauge than the outside diameter of the copper pipe, and the hole we bored had to be dead centre down the length of wood. If you drilled off centre the bit came out the side of the block and it was spoiled.

After successful drilling, the copper tube was hammered through the block until it was flush with the top. The block and excess copper pipe were then cut squarely to the exact length of the minnow required. Being slightly wider than the hole in the block, the copper was jammed and didn't need to be glued. Very few of the copper pipes in our minnows ever came loose or fell out.

A problem arose – how could we fix the block into the lathe so that it would turn and yet leave clearance for the chisel to shape the head end of the lure? Steve came up with the answer. We got an old centre punch and cut off the thick end, leaving us with the tapered end leading to the punch head. The thicker end was locked into the chuck and the copper tube was slid up the taper until it jammed. The other end of the lure was fixed into the tapered head of the tail stock. This was adjusted lengthways until the lathe, when turned on, had sufficient friction on the lure for the chisel to do its work. The lure was shaped, sandpapered and, before being removed from the lathe, two cuts were made with a hacksaw for the later insertion of the fins. I recall that the shape of the first few efforts bore no resemblance to what I reckoned minnows should look like. But after a bit of practise we were turning out nicely shaped lures.

Painting came next, after the fins were glued in. The small spaces at the end of the fin slots were filled with putty and we painted the lure with a wood sealant, then an undercoat of the main colour and a further coat of the main colour in gloss paint. This was followed by the contrast colour, also in gloss paint. After all this the eyes had to be painted on. Heaven knows why because no fish ever saw the eyes on a spinning devon! The whole lure was finished in a coat of clear polyurethane varnish. All this painting was done by hand and it seemed to take for ever. We soon had more devons than we could ever use ourselves and began to sell them to the lads on the river. I remember that we charged 1/9d for each devon shell.

All this happened in early 1965 and we were planning, once the season closed, to get into minnow making in a more serious way and try to streamline the process. But this was when fate dealt a cruel blow. On the 9th of September that year Steve, in his prime at the age of 27, was killed.

I was devastated, of course, and it was a while before I even thought about tackle making. But later, when Steve's things were being sorted out, I took the lathe home to my garage and continued to make wooden devons over the next few years. It was still a painfully slow process. I remember managing to make the huge number of 48 blanks, from boring to sandpapering the shaped lures, by working one full day of at least 10 hours. They still had to be finned, painted and varnished before they were finished. It doesn't need a mathematician to work out that this was not a lucrative way of spending my off duty hours. But I continued, purely as a hobby.

Enter the Wiggly Woggly

I remember, while fishing the Garry one spring, catching a salmon on a Kynoch Killer lure which has a concave shaped head that causes it to dig into the water and dive deeper the harder it is pulled. I began to experiment with lathe-turned lures with slanted heads and each time I went fishing I had a pocketful of prototypes to test. I soon realised that the mechanics of the Kynoch Killer, in which the angle of retrieve was at right angles to the concave head, was totally different to the type of lure I was trying to make. In my lure, which had a conventional devon mount, the angle of retrieve was straight through the body, irrespective of the angled head, and the best movement I could get was a slight wobble.

One day, however, when fishing Lower Dochfour – again courtesy of the late Louis Davidson – I realised that the lure hook, fixed into a tulip bead, was quite rigid. When I substituted the tulip for a split ring, the treble swung from side to side as the lure was being retrieved, improving its action. I made up one of these new lures, about 3½ inches long, and painted it like the Rapala which I had used for many years with great success – white belly, gold flank and black back and, of course, two eyes.

For the next few weeks I fished the new lure every time I went out. I found that, contrary to the Kynoch's action – to go deeper the harder it was retrieved – my lure tended to remain high in the water. One advantage of this was that I could lead-up the mount and, with no fins, it cast like a bullet. Very long casts could be obtained and it kept high in the water during the retrieve.

The first fish I landed on the lure was a kelt but one day, while fishing Dochfour's Culbuie Pool – one of the widest pools on the Ness – I hooked and landed two fish weighing 10 and 25 pounds. This convinced me that the kelt had been no fluke. I called my new lure the Wiggly Woggly after its action and thought that I might be on to something! I began to make enquiries as to how I could go about taking out a patent on this lure.

The move to plastic

This is where fate took a hand and completely changed my tackle making future. I called at Grahams and, after showing Bill Brown my prototype Wiggly Woggly, I asked him if he knew how to go about taking out a patent on it. Bill said, "Why don't you go and see Roland Hill?" I had never heard of this man and told Bill this. He revealed that Roland Hill was running Lochardil Plastics and was the man who had invented the Strathallan Devon. It was a one-piece plastic devon which was unique in that it had glass eyes glued on to it. Indeed, I knew the Strathallan with which I had caught several salmon.

I went up to see Roland, who lived in the Lochardil area of Inverness not far from where I then stayed. Thus began a good, but unfortunately very short, friendship. I showed him my prototype lure and told him how successful it had been for me. We sat and talked for ages and he then said he would give me £100 for it. I was taken aback as this was an awful lot of money then. After thinking about it for a while I suggested that, instead of giving me £100, we should develop the making of the lure together, dividing any expenditure and, if it took off, dividing the proceeds. He told me that he would first have to contact a friend who was a mould maker. After getting the mould he would arrange to make the lures.

My prototype was slightly the worse for wear after all the use I had given it and I arranged to make another from which the mould could be made. Over the next few months I called on Roland and we enjoyed each other's company over a few beers in the Lochardil Hotel. I was told that, due to commitments, the mould making had been put on hold, but he hoped the work would be undertaken within the next few months.

I saw Roland regularly until, one day when I was on duty at the police station, one of my colleagues told me that he had never

ever seen so many minnows as he had seen that day. This garage was filled with minnows, painted and unpainted, from front to back. I asked him where this had been and he told me that he had been attending a sudden death in the Lochardil area of the town and the garage was at this address. I realised that this just had to be Roland Hill! Very shocked, I asked my colleague if he had seen Roland's two Siamese cats which were his inseparable companions. He told me he had not seen them, so I drove up there to enquire after their wellbeing.

The first thing I saw when I arrived were the two cats wandering aimlessly in the front garden. A neighbour kindly agreed to look after them. I then met a gentleman who introduced himself as Roland's brother who had travelled up from Southampton to attend to matters. I offered my condolences to him and we then had a long discussion about Roland and his past. He had been, without question, a very clever man, no matter what he turned his hand to over his working years.

Taking the bull by the horns I told Roland's brother of our 'almost business' connection. While I appreciated that it was not exactly the proper time or place, I asked him — as I would never meet him again — if he would please note my interest in buying some of Roland's manufacturing gear?

That, I thought, was that. Roland's funeral was a private affair and I honestly believed that I would never hear any more about it. Many months later, however, I received a telephone call from a very good friend Sydney Wilson who, by pure coincidence, was a close friend of the person to whom Roland had left all of his estate. Sydney had been informed that my interest had been noted with regard to the fishing lure machinery and moulds and he asked me to make an offer for them.

Thinking it over very quickly, I made an offer of as much as I could afford, bearing in mind that I had never seen the manufacturing side of Roland's lures. It really was a pig in a poke situation. My offer was accepted and a couple of days later I arrived at Roland's house with a couple of pals and a van. We had some struggle lifting the heavy machinery from the garage to the van and then down to my shed, where I installed it in the manner in which I had first seen it.

I had never seen an injection moulding machine working. Enquiries in Inverness at that time revealed there was no such animal up here so I really was in a quandary. It was a case of trial and error but − after many fortunately non-self harming accidents (the plastic melts until literally red hot) − I eventually made my first minnow. I continued to make many more mistakes but managed to mould a sufficient number of minnows to justify bringing the spray gun, also part of the lot, into use. It was so much quicker than hand painting.

Over the next few years I sold quite a few of these lures, two to three inches in size, to various tackle shops in Scotland. I traded these under the company name of MacLures of Inverness. Although there were problems with plastics and specialist paint supplies which I managed to solve, the part-time business was going well. But I wasn't too happy with the lure style itself. There were no glass eyes for them in the gear I had bought but I easily got round that by buffing off the raised eyes on the moulds and painting eyes on the finished lures instead. The biggest problem was that the fins on the one piece moulded lures chipped due to hitting rocks as they were being spun in the river. After a while, the lure just didn't look too well and it didn't spin well either.

The Aswood is born

My favourite lure was still my old faithful, the wooden devon. One day a thought came to me, "Why not make a plastic devon that looks the same, weighs the same and has clear fins like a wooden devon?" I experimented making moulds in plastic and metal, and even tried plaster of paris (which was a complete waste of time). I did manage to turn out the odd lure but it still had to be finished on the lathe. This just wasn't working. Then one summer I met Alva Parkes and his wife Gladys. They came from the West Midlands and had been coming up to fish the Ness every summer for at least ten years. Alva wanted me to tie him some small Black Shrimps which, at that time, were doing very well on the association water.

During our conversation (funny how it happens!), we were talking about minnows and I told him about the difficulty I was having in trying to make moulds. It transpired that Alva just happened to be a tool maker to trade and that mould making was right up his street. The end result was that, thanks to Alva, the Aswood Devon – as I chose to call my new lure – was born. Over the years, I personally have now caught many hundreds of salmon on the lures which I make from 1½ inches through to the four inch trolling special. A high percentage of all the locally caught salmon on spinner are taken on these lures. Incidentally, Alva also made me moulds for my Wiggly Woggly lures, in sizes 2½ inch and 3½ inch. I renamed them the Darter and they have been successful on both river and loch.

Today, I have pretty well closed down the minnow-making business. The machine which has kept going all those years – a miracle in itself – and for which there is no possibility of getting spares, is pretty well worn out. It really served me well and repaid the gamble I took when I first bought it.

For a while I seriously considered going into tackle manufacturing full time after I retired, employing a number of ladies part time who had previously been trained in fly tying at a factory located in the Longman Industrial Estate. The two main fly tyers were Gladys Falconer and Carol Thomson. Goodness knows how many trout and salmon flies they made between them. But failing eyesight, cheap imports and more efficient minnow manufacturing companies made me realise that I could not possibly compete in this field. I have carried on making minnows as no more than a hobby. I still prefer to fish my Aswoods rather than any of the opposition's lures and I do know that, locally at least, so do many other anglers.

Another big fish dwarfs my younger son Paul

22

Germany again

In 1986 my wife and I drove via Hull to Rotterdam heading for Bavaria where we intended to spend the next two weeks touring about. As we would be passing not too far from Wegberg, I thought I would look up the Kutski's, my friends from my RAF days.

I found the RAF hospital without too much difficulty but got stuck when I began to look for my old friends' house. The whole area, which in 1955 had all been fields, was now practically all houses. After wandering around aimlessly for a while I stopped and sought help from a local who was working in his garden.

My German, which was never good but had always got me by in the past, was a bit rusty, to say the least. But I asked the local man if he could tell me where Willy Kutski, who used to work in the Britishi Crankenhaus (British hospital), lived. I'll never forget his reply – translated. "Small man, fair hair? Oh, he emigrated to Canada last year." I was very disappointed as I would have loved to have met them both again. That's life.

After visiting many Bavarian tourist spots and driving as far as Garmish Partinkirchen we intended to complete the holiday by driving down the wine regions of the Rhine. As we approached the small village of Peiting I was hit by a searing pain in my lower belly. Oh, I thought, that was the Schwein cutlets I ate last night. I've got food poisoning! We happened to be passing an industrial site like a quarry and I stopped there where a concerned worker approached the car and asked what was wrong as I looked ill. I replied that I thought I was going to be sick and asked if I could use their toilet. He led me to a building where he opened the door to the toilet. The first thing that struck me, despite being in agony, was the cleanliness of the place. I'm sure it was not what you would find in a quarry toilet over here.

The pain, if anything, got worse and I couldn't be sick. When I came out I asked the man, who was still hovering about outside, if there was a doctor in the house. There was nobody of the medical profession there and he suggested that, if I followed him, he would direct us to the doctor's surgery in the village. By this time, I was almost doubled up in pain but poor Anna couldn't drive on the wrong side of the road. I had to drive, believe me with some difficulty, and followed the man to a street where I saw the doctor's surgery.

The language problem continued as none of the staff, including the doctor, could speak English. All I could tell them was I had a very bad pain, indicating my lower left side opposite the appendix. The doctor, after poking and prodding me, said I would have to go to hospital. I asked him how far away it was. He told me that it was in the next town, Schongau (twinned with Elgin), but I cannot remember how far he said it was.

Obviously, it was too far for me to drive as, by this time, I was writhing in pain. I suggested a taxi, which was arranged and arrived shortly afterwards. After getting Anna to write down the name of the street where we had to leave the car, we were driven to this lovely new hospital built on top of a hill just outside the old walled town.

Once inside, I was examined by another doctor who, again, had no English. However, he told me that my problem was "….. stein." I knew 'stein' meant stone so I suggested, "Kidney stone?" He didn't understand that so, thinking back to my medic days, I wondered what else I could suggest. I remembered that the renal system was connected to the kidneys and suggested, "Renal stein?" This got a thumbs up from the doctor and I was then sure that what was bothering me was kidney stones. I'm sure he called them 'neiren steins'.

I was still in terrible pain and it was only after they put me on a drip that I became much more comfortable. A while after that, with Anna still sitting beside my bed in shorts and a blouse, the doctor came back and said, "Kein angst. Klein operation (Don't worry. Small operation)." But I misunderstood and thought he had said, "Kein operation (No operation)." You can see how I made this wee mistake!

But it wasn't long before I got the message and realised that I would be spending the night, at least, in hospital. In my best German I asked the staff if there was any accommodation for my wife and was told that this facility did not exist. What to do then? I was stuck in bed with a drip in my arm. Fortunately there was a mobile phone available and I had taken a business card from the taxi driver. I had contact with the outside world! I phoned the gentleman and explained the situation to him as best I could, asking him to take Anna to a conveniently situated hotel (where they spoke English) and, most importantly, not too expensive as I didn't know how long I was going to be there. As it was almost the end of the holiday, most of our money had gone.

Anna then left me to go out into the dark – it was now after 9 pm – to meet a total stranger. I can only imagine what she was thinking. But the taxi driver was a real gentleman. He took her to a hotel where the receptionist spoke perfect English. Then, via the receptionist, he persuaded Anna to hand over our car keys, saying that he would take the car to his garage for safe keeping. Anna called me later to ask if she had done the wrong thing! I was drugged to the eyeballs, of course, and couldn't care less.

The next day, before I was taken down to theatre, I recall listening to the three female and one male nurse being briefed by their sister on their tasks for the day. I remember hearing the male nurse, when he was told he had to prep me for theatre, say, "Oh, wunderbaar!"

Shortly before I was taken from the ward to go to theatre, Anna came in and told me that the taxi driver had called at her hotel and had driven her past his garage where he showed her our car safely parked there. He had then taken her to a 'zimmer frei' (room free) or bed and breakfast as they call it there. After she had left her bag there he had driven her to the hospital and hadn't asked for any money. I was impressed!

My operation went OK, but I wouldn't recommend it. I then learned that I would not be discharged from hospital for another two days. Clearly, I couldn't drive the six hundred miles to Rotterdam, nor could Anna, before the day our return booking had been made for us. We were marooned.

I then phoned home and spoke to Anna's eldest daughter Mairi — quite an organiser! — and asked her to tell my youngest son Paul (you will have gathered that we had each been married before) to go to his grandmother, borrow some money and go to the Post Office to get a quickie passport. Mairi arranged for the single air flight to Munchen — Munich to us — and instructed Paul to then go to the Bahnhoff (railway station) and catch a train to Shongau where we would meet him. That gave us just the day after he arrived to drive to Rotterdam — cutting it very fine, I thought!

While this was going on I was discharged from hospital and the same taxi driver picked us up and dropped us at the bed and breakfast. I thanked him profusely for the great assistance he had been to us, particularly to Anna, and paid him what he said was due plus a generous tip. Later that day I collected our car from his garage which was just across the street.

We had the remainder of that day to ourselves. The owner of the bed and breakfast and I had a long blether (I don't know what you call that in pidgin German!) and, surprise, the word fish came up. I learned that he had a couple of ponds with rainbow trout in them and that he was planning to go there that very afternoon with his grandson to catch some. He invited us to accompany them. We drove in his big Mercedes estate car a few miles out of the town and stopped beside two ponds which were perhaps 40 feet square. There was no sign of life in them until he threw in some pellets, when the surface of the ponds just boiled. The grandson, who was about 10 years old, had a small glass fibre spinning rod with matching reel and line and a small silver Mepps-type lure. He didn't have much of an idea how to use it so, of course, I felt I had to give him a hand. It certainly wasn't fishing as I know it but the wee laddie had a ball pulling in hard-fighting rainbow trout. Each weighed about two pounds. I have to admit I also caught one or two.

That evening Anna and I went down to the local railway station and waited for Paul to arrive. I had almost given up hope of seeing him when he came off another train minutes after the one I expected him from had come and gone. I never was very good at reading German timetables! We took Paul for a quick run round Schongau and, after giving him his first taste of real German beer, we went off to bed.

The next morning we began our long journey north. Paul had never ever been south of Perth and, obviously, driving on the wrong side of the road was new to him. Most of the roads we drove on were autobahns and the miles just melted away. We made one mistake, finding ourselves on an exit lane into a large city – Stuttgart, I think – but we managed, God knows how, to find ourselves back on the correct route north again.

Approaching Rotterdam less than 20 minutes before our ferry departure time was a real experience. All the jetties are called

Havens and what a job we had finding the one from which our ship would be leaving. When we eventually found it all the cars and then the lorries and buses had embarked but the gates were still open. I ran across to one of the officials there, showed him our boarding papers and he waved us on. Minutes later the gates closed – they had been waiting for us! – and we sailed off. We went straight to the bar and had a couple of stiff ones which I felt we really deserved.

The one advantage of being last on was that we were first off the next morning. The Customs men, clearly expecting buses and lorries, just waved us straight through. The journey home was fast and uneventful. Paul performed far better than I thought he would.

The end result of this is that Anna will not go on a foreign driving holiday again. I can't understand why?

23

Ghillying

On many occasions over the years, particularly when I was fishing with Mrs Boyd on the Findhorn and the Ness, I would act as her ghillie. This did not just entail standing watching her fish. I always checked the cast, renewed it if necessary and tied on the flies. Obviously, if a fish was hooked I would net it, remove the hook and, after checking the cast again, give her back the rod so that she could continue fishing. Mrs Boyd had been fishing much longer than I had been alive and I wouldn't have considered giving her any advice unless she asked me.

On the Ness Mrs Boyd always fished from a boat where I felt I had more control over how she fished. The boat was always anchored and we fished down the pool by letting out the rope attached to the anchor. Like most other boat anglers Mrs Boyd would cast a fixed length of line. I could position the boat so that I knew her fly would be covering the fish I had seen move earlier, or the lie which was out of her normal range.

I had the pleasure of acting as ghillie for many people and usually, depending on the number of fish in the river and the anglers' abilities, had varying success. If no fish were taken by the end of the day I was just as disappointed as the angler, but if we had a good day and landed fish we both made our way back from the river feeling good – and the tip was usually that bit better too!

I have had the pleasure, many times, to act as ghillie for Lords and Ladies, and also commoners, but one day stands out among them all. It wasn't because of the fish we caught, for we caught none, but the circumstances were a bit out of the normal.

One day my friend Roddy Forbes, the head ghillie at Lord Cawdor's Estate, phoned me to ask if I could ghillie for a guest the following afternoon. I was free and arranged with Roddy to meet up with the guest at Drynachan Lodge. Roddy asked that I bring a rod with me for use by the guest.

I was early in arriving at Drynachan the next afternoon. Shortly afterwards, a convoy of vehicles led by Roddy in his Land Rover pulled up. The Dowager Angelica got out of the second vehicle and a man who was immediately familiar to me – it was Prince Michael, Duke of Kent – got out of the third car. After the formalities were dispensed with, the Dowager Angelica asked me if I could ensure that the Duke of Kent was back at the castle in time for dinner at seven pm. I was told to take the guest up to the top beat which involved fording the river and driving about a mile up a narrow rough track, part of which passes high over the top of the precipitous bank of one of the pools.

Prince Michael was driving with his personal bodyguard beside him and I and my trusty old Labrador Ilé got in the back of his latest model Range Rover. I held the assembled rod out of the open window and off we set.

I directed the Prince on the way to go and when we came to the ford across the river I did expect him to slow down a bit. But he was having none of it and we crossed the river at the fastest speed I guarantee it had ever been crossed. Prior to reaching the part high above the river, I did point out the narrowness of the track – hoping that he would slow down a bit – but we carried on at the same breakneck speed and were soon parking at the pool where I had decided we should start fishing.

When we got out of the car it began to rain and the Prince pulled on a smart new wax jacket. The bodyguard remained in the car. When I asked my charge where his waders were he said he had been told he would not need any. To fish this particular pool, and indeed most of the pools on the river, it is necessary to at least get one's feet wet, so I had a bit of a quandary. What could I do? I couldn't go back to my car to get my shoes so I asked him what was his foot size. He replied, "Nine and a half, I think." I am a size 10 so I took my waders off and put on his size nine and a half Saville Row shoes. That was a first for sure!

The Prince had obviously never fished before but after giving him a few basic tips on how to cast and handline, he was soon casting adequately over the water which had a good number of old coloured fish showing in it. These fish gave him the incentive to fish on all afternoon and, at six pm, I had to remind him of the time and the fact that he was to be back at the castle for dinner at seven pm. His reply was, "Just another five minutes, John." Unfortunately there was no happy ending to our afternoon's fishing, but I am certain he enjoyed it.

On my numerous visits to various rivers, the beats I fished had resident ghillies. I didn't really require their services although their presence on the river bank was pleasant and many happy stories were swapped. Among the ghillies I became very friendly with were James MacDonnell, River Moriston; Bill Paton and Robin MacLeod, Dochfour Beat, River Ness; Jack Falconer, Laggan Beat, River Ness; Murdo MacKintosh and Dave Stewart Ness Castle Beat, River Ness; Harry Fraser and Scottie MacKenzie, Ness Side Beat, River Ness; Colin Reid and John Whyte, Brae Water Beats, River Spey; and Tom Hay, Grantully Beat, River Tay.

British record brown trout

Keith misses out

In 1963 I learned that local angler Keith Norris had caught a very large brown trout in Loch Killin, near Whitebridge, Inverness-shire, a loch renowned for its five to the pound brownies and small char. The word was that it weighed over 10 pounds. At that time I was writing my weekly 'Black Shrimp' angling column in the Highland News and thought this would make a good story. I contacted Keith expecting to be told that the trout had been eaten, but learned that it was still in his freezer.

I arranged for Keith to take it down to his shop where I could see it. Arriving there the next day I got the shock of my life when I looked in a black bin liner and saw this fish, still partly frozen. This was no 10 pounder! Keith told me that when he had taken the fish home after catching it a fortnight earlier, it had weighed over 19 pounds on spring balance scales. This would have been a new British record had it been weighed and witnessed accurately at that time. I sent Keith to the nearby butcher's shop to have it properly weighed. On his return he told me it weighed 17½ pounds, not including the ice water in the bag. By not knowing the proper procedure to follow poor Keith had lost out on claiming the British record.

I took scales from Keith's fish and sent them to the Freshwater Fisheries Laboratory at Faskally, near Pitlochry. These showed the fish to be 22 to 23 years old which, I understand, is the oldest brown trout ever recorded.

What might have been – Keith Norris with his 17½ pound brown trout

Jim's Dream Trip

I'll never forget the day of the first ever Highland Field Sports Fair held in the grounds of Lord Burton's estate at Dochfour, near Inverness, in 1978. Inverness Angling Club had a tent with exhibitions of fishing tackle and casting competitions for trout accuracy and salmon distance, and I was helping out.

Rain threatened that day and I was coming back from the car park, having retrieved my jacket from the car, when I saw a couple I recognised but, at that time, did not know well – Jim and Betty Jackson who then ran the Spar shop in the Hilton area of Inverness. Jim gave me a call and when I went over to speak to him he asked if I would verify a fish for him. I immediately thought that he had been sea fishing and, perhaps, had caught a pollack or a saithe, which are quite similar in appearance, and wanted me to identify the species. Indicating I would be glad to do so, I asked what kind of fish it was. He replied, "A 20 pound brown trout."

To say the least, I was a bit taken aback as I was aware that the British record for the species then stood at 18½ pounds from Loch Garry. I thought that, in all probability, the weight had been guessed or exaggerated. When I asked, he told me that he had weighed it the evening before on a spring balance which showed that it was 21 pounds. I suggested that the scales were inaccurate but he told me he had weighed it on his certificated shop scales that morning and it had scaled 19 pounds 9 ounces 4 grams.

By now I was very excited indeed – a new British record and I was going to be one of the first to see it! "Where is the fish, Jim?" I asked. He replied, "In the boot of my car," indicating his car just behind him in the car park. I just couldn't wait to see it and, when he opened the boot, there was 'Fred' as we called it thereafter – a beautifully shaped monster with heavily spotted markings.

Jim told me that, the previous day, he had been fishing Loch Quoich at the head of the Garry system with his eight-year-old son Graham. They had been trolling away without any luck when Jim had decided to turn round and go back in the opposite direction. He had carried out this manoeuvre in the middle of the loch without first retrieving the lure, allowing it to sink deep into the loch. When the line tightened up again the fish was on!

He had played it from the boat for quite some time and then, realising its size, had gone ashore to land it.

The fish had been put into the bottom of the boat under a jacket for the rest of the day and only weighed when they got home late that evening. A fish of this size, left under a jacket in the hot sunny conditions of the previous day and overnight before being properly weighed, would have definitely lost at least one pound in weight. Goodness knows what the true weight of it would have been!

Prize fish – Jimmy Jackson with his British record brown trout

When I asked Jim what lure he had caught it on, he said, "One of those Mepp-type spoons – no, a Droppen." I realised then that, as the lure he had taken the fish on was produced by Abu and the fish was unquestionably going to be ratified as a new British record, he would qualify as a winner in the Swedish fishing tackle company's annual Dream Trip competition. Jim said he thought it might qualify for the Fish of the Week competition in one of the Sunday newspapers. But I assured him that he was really into the big time with Fred.

I took the fish down to Fishermen's Corner where it was on display on ice for the two days of the fair. The comments from gamekeepers, ghillies and anglers were hilarious. "That's not a trout, they don't grow that big!" – and many more. In the meantime I had photographed Fred and taken scales from him before making application, on Jim's behalf, to have the record ratified.

The scales were forwarded to the Freshwater Fisheries Laboratory at Faskally, near Pitlochry, and I later learned from them that Fred was a male brown trout aged 12. I put in an application to Abu on Jim's behalf for the brown trout winner of the Dream Trip competition and Jim later enjoyed an all expenses paid trip to Mexico fishing for swordfish and other exotic species. A Dream Trip indeed!

So what happened to Fred? Jim made several fibre glass casts of the fish which I painted and mounted. One is in Jim's house, another in the Glen Affric Hotel at Cannich, one is in the Clachnaharry Inn in Inverness and the fourth is in the Steading Hotel and Restaurant in Strathnairn. Fred's remains were forwarded to Faskally to assist in their research into big trout.

Jim's record was subsequently beaten by a large fish from one of the Irish loughs. I often wonder how much heavier Jim's Fred might have been if it had lived as long as Keith's trout, almost twice the age.

New record awaited

Large brown trout exist in many of our local lochs like Lochs Ness, Garry, Ericht and Killin. These fish are exactly the same species as the five-to-the-pound variety which can be caught in many of our hill lochs but for some reason they turn completely cannibal and increase weight dramatically. These fish are known as ferox. It is only on the very odd occasion they rise to a fly so the only real chance of catching them is on bait or deeply fished spun lures.

In the case of Lochs Ness and Killin the staple diet of these fish is, without doubt, the Artic char which are known to live in these lochs. This species has survived since the Ice Age and live in shoals at depths of 80 to 100 feet. They are identical in shape and fin formation to trout but are usually greenish in colour with white spots. I am certain that char exist in Lochs Garry and Quoich. After all, they are also part of the Ness system and huge brown trout have also been caught in these lochs.

I firmly believe that ferox of possibly up to 30 pounds, perhaps even heavier, live in some of our deeper Highland lochs, including Loch Shin which has regularly yielded double figure ferox. It is just a matter of time, I believe, before a new British record brown trout is caught in our part of Scotland.

25

Long cast

Thanks to Mr Herd, the then owner of the Garry Fishings, I went there on a March day in the 1970s taking with me my pals Alan Scott and Gordon Smith. They had not fished these waters before and both were looking forward to the day there.

At that time of the season, all the fishing was done in the estuary beat of the river where the Garry enters Loch Oich, and in Loch Oich itself by boat. The reason for this was that the Hydro didn't release water to run from the dam down to the loch until April. The spring fish were held up in the estuary until the water came when they could begin to make their way towards the spawning grounds further up the system.

Many years ago, in order to improve the fishing in the lower part of the river where it joins the loch, the proprietors built a long narrow earthen extension into the loch on the south side of the river. This concentrated the river into a narrow funnel and provided an extra 50 yards of bank fishing on both sides. On my many visits to the Garry, I fished from both the north bank and from the spit, as the new bank was called. Of the fish I caught from the estuary beat, most came from the spit.

On this particular day, Gordon was rowed across to the spit to try spinning and Alan and I decided to fish the north bank. Alan was Speycasting away with his home-built 14 foot rod, a floating line and a Silver Wilkinson single. The north bank is a bit awkward to cast from and he wasn't able to get further than about one third of the way across the pool. I was spinning in front of Alan and we fished away for quite a while with no success. Gordon, having reached the end of the spit, cast across too close to where Alan was standing, and across his line. There was an immediate shout from Alan. I realised that Gordon had hooked Alan's line and he had initially thought he was into a fish.

After a few moments of indecision Gordon shouted that he would wind in Alan's line, bringing the fly line across the full 60 yard width of the river. Gordon unhooked his line from Alan's cast, held the fly up clear of the bank and dropped it back into the water. Alan began to wind in his line but, as he later told us, "Why not take advantage of the fact that my fly is right at the other side of the river? I'll just let it fish all the way across to my side."

That is what he did but the fly never reached his side of the river. A salmon grabbed it and after quite a tussle I netted a lovely, clean run 11 pounder for a more than delighted Alan. It just shows that the long cast does result in a hooked fish. Sometimes!

Product of a long cast – Alan Scott with his 11 pound Garry fish

26

Sea fishing

Another branch of the sport is sea fishing which I was lucky enough to be involved in back in the days when fish were plentiful – long before klondykers dropped anchor in Loch Broom and processed fish there by the ton!

My first venture into sea angling was way back in the late 1960s, I guess, when I got together with Rod Michie, the then manager of the Muirtown Motel; the late Jimmy Strachan; Duncan MacKintosh, the taxi driver; and Calum Lamont of the Highlands and Islands Development Board.

Ullapool was our destination and we fished from an old clinker-built boat powered by an old Seagull motor. We had some great sport, fishing just off Ullapool and in Ardmair Bay where we landed haddock, whiting, mackerel, dog fish, saithe and an occasional thornback skate. We never came home without good baskets of fish. The only trouble was that this was in the days before most houses had deep freezers and a lot of the fish went to waste.

Later on we used to charter larger boats which Ullapool fishermen such as Murdo Simon hired out to fishing parties. We could then venture further afield to off Achiltibuie and the Summer Isles. I used to take my late brother-in-law Mick Stone, from Guildford, my sons and many police colleagues on trips and some really wonderful days were enjoyed there.

Moving with the times

The sea fishing generally became very poor and I gave up this branch of the sport for many years. In about 2000, however, I joined the Leachkin Sea Angling Club of Inverness and had many outings with them to Scrabster, Lochinver and Kinlochbervie.

I was impressed by the way the modern sea angler has changed his techniques since my early days at the game. A set of white feathers, sometimes baited with a piece of mackerel, sufficed for catching all the fish then, but now I was amazed to see each hook supplemented with up to half a dozen coloured beads and often with large spoons above. But boy, did this new method work, particularly with cod! Until I changed my gear from the old fashioned white feathers to the modern rigs, I did not catch nearly as many fish as my companions. I don't think it's because the fish have become more sophisticated: they have become much fewer and are more readily tempted by colourful, flashing rigs.

I still manage a day or two sea fishing out from Lochinver where our skipper Bruce MacKenzie always does his best to find fish for us. But for whatever the reason – global warming is often blamed – the haddock are no longer there. Yet it was only eight to ten years ago when we could fill a box each of prime haddies. Fortunately there is still a small number of codling about and they make a nice fry-up too!

Arthur loses his cool

For a number of years, until its recent disbandment, I was a member of the Thistle Angling Club in Inverness organised by Arthur Fraser, who at that time ran a hairdresser's business in Inverness Market Arcade. I enjoyed some very happy outings with Arthur, John MacLennan, Bill Doherty, Davie Simpson, John 'The Fish' MacDonald and Tony McCall, fishing out of Gairloch, Lochinver and Helmsdale. It was only a small club but we did enjoy the trips.

On each trip the club ran competitions for the heaviest fish, heaviest basket and greatest number of species. These were keenly contested. I'll never forget one hilarious trip to Helmsdale where, as the known lies are only a few hundred yards offshore, we began fishing within a few minutes of leaving the harbour.

Arthur was the first to land a nice cod of perhaps six pounds which he put into a black polythene bag and left it under his seat. It was a particularly hot day and most of the lads kept their catch cool by frequently throwing buckets of water over their fish. But Arthur must have forgotten his fish, or he was too busy trying to catch another, for he failed to keep his catch cool. His fish ended up being his only catch of the day.

Come weigh-in at the end of the day, the other rods had caught more fish but Arthur's cod was by far the heaviest landed. As he went to take the fish out of the bag to weigh it, I'll never forget what happened next. He put his hand inside the bag and grabbed his fish by the tail. But when he lifted it from the bag all the flesh fell from the carcase and he was left holding the fish's tail, spine and head. It was, if anything, slightly overcooked!

Seal steals the show

The only other place I manage to go sea fishing is when I go to Islay every year so that my wife can get her annual shot in the arm of her birthplace. At Port Ellen, where we always stay, my friend and well-known fisherman Alec Campbell always takes me out for an evening or two fishing off the rocks at the Mull of Oa, where we usually catch a fair number of saithe and lythe, and plenty of mackerel in season. At Port Ellen pier there is a tame seal which amuses the tourists and kids most evenings in the summer. He will come several feet out of the water to grab a mackerel held out from a boat for him.

The intelligence of seals was really brought home to me a few years ago by an experience while fishing out of Scrabster with the Leachkin club boys. Ten of us were fishing from the boat and we were all after cod. Several of the experts soon had some nice ones on board and the rest of us just waited our turn. Some small ones were landed and the boys put them head first into a bucket to keep them alive. This was just in case an opportunity arose to try for a shark which they apparently catch up there, although I have never seen one.

That's when things started to go wrong! Every time someone hooked a cod, and just when it had been wound in half way to the surface, something grabbed it and took off. Some of the lads thought it might be a shark but that was eliminated as the culprit when, as one lad's line was being pulled strongly away from the boat, it began to rise to the surface. There was his Christmas tree rig with a nice cod attached – held in the mouth of a big seal! The line, of course, soon broke. I think everyone in the boat, including myself, lost fish to this seal that afternoon. The skipper moved the boat but, as soon as someone hooked a fish, there was the seal again – proving that he had followed the boat.

One of the boys had his shark rod with him and thought he would have a bit of sport. He fitted up his rod with a steel trace and size 8/0 hook, hooked one of the live codlings through the mouth and out the side of its gills, and dropped it over the side. It was a lovely calm day and we all watched as the bait sank deeper and deeper in the water. Then a huge greenish blue object appeared, the bait disappeared and the reel began to run. After a few seconds the drag was put on and the reel began to scream – not for long, though, as the line suddenly went slack. When the line was wound in there was the cod's head. The rest of its body had been neatly nipped off.

A different approach was needed so the next bait fish was hooked in the tail and the procedure followed as before. We watched until we saw the big flash and then the reel screamed and went slack again. On retrieval, it was found that this time the seal had left us the cod's tail and the hook. In another attempt to fool the old seal, the hook was put through the middle of the back of the cod. This time – after the take, the run, the slack line and the retrieval – what had the seal left us? Yes, you're right, the middle cut of the cod! That animal was so experienced, no doubt after a long apprenticeship, that it could identify the hook and eat all round it without becoming hooked. I'll bet it's sorry when the close season comes!

27

Strangest things I have ever hooked

When you go fishing you hope, naturally, that fish will be what you hook. But in my many years of experience I have managed on quite a few occasions to hook something unexpected.

One day, when I was still using my Malloch spinning reel, I was standing at the top of the Black Stream beside Inverness Cathedral casting a number five Phantom, a canvas-bodied lure weighted with lead shot and armed with three size four trebles. I got a strike, immediately struck back and began to try to bring in what I thought must be a salmon because of its strength. But then the line went up and up into the air!

At first I could not understand what was going on but then realised that two seagulls, behaving very unnaturally in the air, were in fact hooked and tangled in my line. One gull had grabbed the lure and hooked itself while the other had flown into the line, catching its wings. I had a real struggle before I could bring these birds in close enough to unhook. During this time both were pecking at me for all they were worth, leaving me with scratches and bites on both hands.

The next time I connected with a gull was while I was night fishing for sea trout on the Ness. The trout are generally caught during the short-lived rise of natural flies just after darkness has fallen. This can last for up to half an hour and after that the trout generally go off the take.

The rise had just commenced and I soon caught a nice trout. After landing it, and on the very next cast, I hooked a gull on the dropper of my two fly cast. I drew the line in under my left arm until I could reach the bird, still protected by my arm. After a struggle I managed to unhook it and dropped it back into the river, in which I was wading waist deep at the time. It floated downstream and promptly hooked itself on the tail hook of the cast, which was dangling in the water. I had no alternative but to go through the whole procedure again. When I eventually began fishing again the rise was off, and I got no further sport that night.

The same experience was almost duplicated a year or two later but this time it was a bat I hooked! I took extreme care to avoid the little devil's sharp teeth.

A bit of a chase

Perhaps the strangest and certainly the heaviest thing I ever hooked was in the 1960s when I was fishing a beat on the River Don with my colleague Bill Cormack. I was fishing a pool where there were so many bushes on the bank that my normal Speycasting was not possible. I was obliged to resort to overhead casting in order to reach the potential lies on the opposite side of the river.

I was casting away quite comfortably until, on the forward cast, the line stopped behind me. "Dash it, I've caught on one of the bushes," I thought, but when I looked I saw this big cow standing there, apparently unconcerned, with a size six Garry Dog stuck in its neck. I thought, "I might be able to retrieve this situation." Holding my rod parallel to the ground and pointed at the cow, I walked slowly towards the beast winding the line in as I went. My intention was to get close to it and pull sharply on the cast, hoping that the fly might pull clear of the poor cow – or, at worst, leave only a short length of cast and the fly!

All went well until I was about 15 to 20 yards away. Then the cow, as if it had received an electric shock, jumped, turned and bolted off across the field. I knew there was no hope of stopping it so I grabbed the line and held on, expecting either the fly to pull out or the cast to break. But it was the line, an old silk one, that snapped and the cow ran off taking over 20 yards of my 30 yard line with it.

I spent ages stalking the cow and diving at the end of the line hoping to catch it before it ran off again. But the best I did was to have the line run through my fingers. Chest waders are not recommended for this athletic pursuit! Before we left I contacted the farmer, who didn't seem too concerned and said that the cow would soon get rid of the hook by rubbing its neck against a fence. Poor fly!

Shot by a swivel

Among the strangest things I have ever hooked I suppose I must include myself. I have hooked different parts of my anatomy, including fingers, ear, neck and lip. Following these mishaps I have had to present myself at the Casualty Departments - first at the old Royal Northern Infirmary and later at Raigmore Hospital – on at least four occasions over the years to have them removed. At least my anti-tetanus injections were kept up to date!

The last occasion I had to go to hospital was as a result of a strange occurrence while I was fishing the Spey near Fochabers. I was accompanied by my nephew Duncan, aged about 16 at the time. He had previously fished with me and was quite competent with a spinning rod.

It had been a very successful day for me, landing some six or seven salmon, so I gave Duncan the rod and sat on the bank to have a rest. The only obstacle to Duncan's fishing was a large tree which was stuck in the middle of the river towards the bottom of the pool. I told Duncan to watch that he didn't cast too far over when he came near the tree and he acknowledged this. On the next cast, however, I heard a cry from Duncan and there he was with my favourite minnow stuck on some debris which was tangled among the tree roots.

I took the rod from him. It was impossible to wade out to the tree and when all efforts to pull the hooks free failed, I told Duncan to turn his back towards the river before I tried to break my line in order to protect his face and eyes should the lure break free and fly towards us with the velocity of a bullet. I did the same and, pointing the rod towards the tree, I began pulling with the intention of either pulling the hook free or breaking the 15 pound line. The only unprotected part of me facing the river was my left little finger. I pulled and pulled and then there was a crack like a rifle shot and I was struck on the left little finger with such velocity that I thought I had been shot!

When I looked I saw that the ball bearing swivel had hit my little finger just above the knuckle and had travelled below the skin and out again next to my ring finger. Both eyes of the swivel were exposed, one on each side of the finger. There was no question of attempting to remove it there. It was the end of the day anyway.

I had a very uncomfortable run home to Inverness, first to drop off Duncan and then up to Casualty at Raigmore to have the swivel surgically removed. I still have the scar!

No mercy from Casualty

Unquestionably, the most painful incident occurred one spring while I was fishing in the Red Braes Pool above the weir in the Ness. I hooked a small fish which was immediately identified as a kelt weighing about five pounds. It was very unceremoniously dragged up the bank away from the water's edge and I knelt down to unhook it. I was using a sprat type lure with a trace of two treble hooks which had been attached to the tail of the lure with some fine wire. As intended, the wire had broken away when the fish took. The fish was hooked on the bottom treble, two inches below the second hook. I placed my left hand over the flank of the fish in order to keep it still and then began to attempt to unhook it using my right hand.

All was going well until the fish flapped violently, as they always do in these circumstances, and I lost my grip of it with my left hand. I quickly withdrew my right hand from the proximity of the fish's mouth but forgot all about the second treble! It was immediately embedded in the top of my middle finger and the fish fell back into the water and tried to swim away. I had no option but to lift the fish bodily from the water with the only point of contact between us being the hook in my finger. Boy, I tell you, that was painful!

I took the hook out of the fish's mouth as quickly as I could, slid it back into the water and turned my attention to the hook in my finger. It was obvious from the angle at which it entered my finger that it was right into the bone and I didn't even try to pull it out. I cut my line and, clasping the whole lure in my right hand, made my way down to the Weir Pool where my old friend Aeneas MacKay was fishing. I asked him if he had a pair of pliers with him and when he asked what I wanted them for I opened my right hand, now bloodied, to show him the lure and hooks.

Poor Aeneas' face blanched and he later told me that he thought I wanted him to pull the hook out of my finger. But all I wanted the pliers for was to cut the trace above the offending hook so that I could better handle my bicycle on my way to the hospital, without the encumbrance of the lure and second treble in my hand.

By the time I got to the old Royal Northern Infirmary my finger was throbbing and extremely painful. I was eventually seen by a young doctor who had obviously never seen a fish hook or knew what it looked like. I tried to explain to him what had happened and suggested that the easiest solution was to make a small incision in my finger to expose the barb and then lift the hook out.

But he had better ideas. His first attempt was to try to push the hook further into my finger until the point and barb came out. I knew that the hook was well embedded in the bone and this would not work. All the time the finger was becoming more swollen and turning black. The pain was something else!

Next he tried to cut the hook using a small hand-held surgical instrument like a tiny circular saw. But all that happened when he tried to cut the old hand made treble, which I had found in an old tackle box while working in Grahams, was that the teeth of this saw just pinged off and the instrument was ruined. He then disappeared from the room and shortly afterwards reappeared with a pair of electrician's pliers which he had borrowed from a 'sparkie' who had been rewiring a room nearby. These did the trick after quite a struggle when I probably yelped like a dog as my finger was pushed this way and that. There was a click and the hook was cut leaving the point, barb and part of the bend still attached.

So what did he do then? He made a small incision, exposed the barb and lifted out what was left of the hook with no problem. A couple of small stitches, trousers down and an anti-tetanus jab and I was allowed to go. If at first he had done what I suggested, I would at least still have had my hook!

28

Foul hooked?

When we hook a salmon or any other game fish we expect to find the hook in or near its mouth. But I have witnessed three instances which, personally, I'd never heard of before.

The first one was when fishing one of the Findhorn beats downstream of Dulsie Bridge. I was fishing alone when I came to a pool with a swirling backwater at the edge of a fast run. I cast over the run several times and then crept down quietly behind a large rock to the side of the run and looked over into the backwater. There I saw a big salmon lying close to my side of the river, facing downstream against the backwater current.

I was using a size 10 Hairy Mary and cast it lightly beyond the fish and shortened line as the fly, carried by the current, approached the fish. The salmon, without apparently moving its body, sucked in the fly which disappeared. I had never witnessed this before and waited for the fish to give me a pull. That's what they normally do, isn't it? But to my astonishment I saw the fish spit out the fly which trundled down the full length of the fish until I cast again. I cast over the fish a good half dozen times more but the fly was ignored. I realised, of course, that I had missed my chance by not striking. As the fish seemed undisturbed I decided to leave it for a while and then give it another try.

Moving downstream, I fished the other pools on the beat for about an hour then returned to the pool where the fish was still in the same position. I cast over it again and slowly handlined until the fly was directly in front of its mouth. Once again I saw the fly being sucked in but this time I struck immediately and hooked the fish. I had a particularly long and difficult time before I was able to land this fish, two pools downstream. It was a beautiful clean run 18 pounder. The hook was embedded at the back of its tongue. I never visited that beat again but I'll bet fish still lie in the same spot.

Another surprising incident also occurred on the Findhorn when I was fishing one of the lower beats by invitation. I had taken with me my friend Dougie Miller who had never fished the Findhorn before. We fished most of the day without an offer but there was a good number of coloured fish showing in most pools.

I watched while Dougie fly fished a particularly deep pool with a swirling backwater on our side of the river. If the line was left too long it sank into this backwater and was difficult to retrieve for the next cast. Preparing for his next cast, Dougie raised his rod and handlined a few yards and shouted, "I'm on, John." I went down with the gaff, waited until he played it out and gaffed a nice freshish 10 pounder. I killed it and turned it on its side to unhook it but could not see any fly in its mouth. I then spotted the hook stuck into one of its pectoral fins with the cast going under the gill cover and out through its mouth. Clearly, the fish had taken the fly on a slack line – because of the backwater – and, not liking what it had tasted, had ejected it back through the gills. I had never witnessed anything like that before.

An even more remarkable incident along the same lines as these previous two stories took place while spring fishing in the River Oich with my pal Bryan Allely. Bryan was spinning some 50 yards downstream of me on one of my favourite pools on this river, Camelon Pool, when he hooked a fish. I ran down to give him a hand. It was soon obvious that the fish he had hooked was a very good one but it was soon played out and I tailed it and laid it on the snow where we admired it.

The fish was clean run with sea lice still sticking to it but it was its shape that we could hardly believe. I have seen very many salmon in my day but I have never seen one which was so fat in relation to its length. It turned out to weigh 20 pounds but, to be honest, 12 pounds would have been a more appropriate weight for its length.

I'm getting away from the point, however. Bryan was fishing with a 2¾ inch yellow belly – a Strathallan original. And where was it hooked? – on the pectoral fin with the line going under the gill cover and out of the fish's mouth!

I can understand a salmon being able to eject a small thing like a size 10 fly through its gills. But a 2¾ inch devon, plus all the associated ironmongery? That must certainly be a first!

29

The Loch Ness Monster

I firmly believe that something – or more likely some things – exist in Loch Ness and also Loch Morar, as I have personally spoken to more than a few people who claim to have seen something most unusual in these waters. I know these people well and I know they were not making up what they saw.

I am aware that seals are often seen in Loch Ness having followed the runs of salmon up the River Ness. These animals – and, perhaps, otters and freak waves – could have convinced watchers that they had seen 'The Monster'. But I believe what the group of people saw in the following story was something that cannot be explained away by seals, otters or a wave. I hope, one day in the not too distant future, some scientific evidence will be found to prove once and for all what species of animal exists in these deep waters.

One story I heard, and verified by speaking to two of the many witnesses, happened in the mid 1970s. Two of my colleagues, a sergeant and a constable then stationed at Fort Augustus, were driving towards Fort Augustus from Drumnadrochit. As they approached Inchnacardoch Hotel they saw a number of cars parked at the side of the road with their passengers pointing excitedly out on to Loch Ness.

The policemen stopped and got out of their car to see what was going on. About halfway across the loch, which was very calm apart from a very slight ripple caused by a light westerly breeze, they saw a hump sticking out of the water. They both likened it to the roof of a VW Beetle car in size but it was distinctly moving westwards against the breeze. It was actually causing a slight wake which, when it reached the shore where all the spectators were standing, made them all step back to avoid getting their feet wet.

The police car, in line with normal practice, carried a camera with which one of the officers took a number of photographs of the 'object'. Soon afterward, it sank beneath the surface and disappeared. It was at this point that my colleagues – clearly, neither of them were experienced photographers – discovered that the lens cap had not been removed from the camera. Trust me, that is true. But I will not name the officers, for obvious reasons! They said, however, there was absolutely no doubt that what they had seen was animate and obviously only part of what was a very large animal indeed.

Around that time frequent articles were appearing in the press stating, for example, that a group of Japanese scientists were coming to Loch Ness to attempt to capture the monster by some fancy means or other. I recall reading one such article which stated that a group of people were going to try catching the monster by using extracts from the sex glands of whales. I didn't give this more than a glance and believed that such efforts were no more than gimmicks to get publicity.

On a day in late March of 1972, however, the police in Inverness were informed that a group had actually managed to catch something. This was verified by several locals who stated they had actually seen a huge dead animal in the back of a van at the side of Loch Ness. Within hours the police switchboard was inundated with telephone calls from just about every newspaper in Britain, and from as far afield as the USA, Japan and even New Zealand.

What is not commonly known is that there is a bye-law, dating back to the 1930s, which "prohibits any person taking or injuring any creature from the waters of Loch Ness." Under the authority of this legislation, a lookout for the vehicle was passed to all Scottish police forces requesting that, if it was traced, it and its occupants be detained.

That evening, we heard that the vehicle and its two male occupants had been stopped at the Forth Road Bridge and taken to Dunfermline Police Station. The vehicle contained a large animal of an unknown species. The late Detective Sergeant Duncan 'Dornie' MacKenzie and I were instructed to travel to Dunfermline to interview the two men, examine the creature and take whatever action we deemed necessary. I was more than excited as I was, and still am, a firm believer in the existence of some unknown animal in Loch Ness. Perhaps these men or their party, I thought, had genuinely captured one of these animals and I was going to be one of the first to see it! The local press were on top of this story, of course, and the evening editions had it that Duncan was a 'photographic expert' and I was 'an expert on wild and marine life'. I don't know where they got that from!

On our arrival in Dunfermline we first interviewed the two men who insisted that they had received a call from their colleagues at Loch Ness stating that they had managed to capture a huge animal in the loch and it had died. They had requested that transport be sent to uplift the animal and take it back south. When asked where they were going to take the animal, they were most reluctant to answer but eventually admitted that they were to have taken it to the Flamingo Land Zoo in North Yorkshire. At this point I was beginning to think there was something not right about the whole affair.

When Duncan and I opened the van and saw the creature for the first time, it didn't look right either. It filled the box van from front to back and side to side and I estimated that it must have weighed three tons, at least. I expected Nessie to have a long neck and small head, as described by many witnesses, but this thing had no neck whatsoever. It had fins at the shoulders and a fin-like tail. Apart from looking not unlike a seal, I didn't know what it was. Meantime, we were awaiting the arrival of the curator of Edinburgh Zoo who had been sent for to see if he could identify the species. When he arrived a short time later and viewed the beast, he identified it as an elephant seal, the whiskers of which had been shaved off!

When confronted by this the two men admitted it had been part of an elaborate hoax. The animal had died at the zoo and someone had dreamt up the idea – if they set the scene by sending up a team to Loch Ness, then apparently catching Nessie and returning it to the zoo – the publicity would have ensured a huge attendance at the zoo and the hoax would only be revealed on the 1st of April. Some April Fool, but I was disappointed that it wasn't the real MacCoy!

Ness Islands and pool names

The Ness Islands are without doubt one of the most popular tourist attractions in Scotland, but something that very few people know today is that in the 1700s all the islands were joined together, bank to bank, by weirs with cruives built into them. The object was to create a huge fish trap where the fish, trapped behind the cruives, could be lifted out of the water. This was an extremely efficient way to trap fish, particularly in low water.

Although the cruives were left open on occasions to let the fish through, the upper proprietors on the river – whose catches were unquestionably affected by these fish traps – had to take legal action against them and, eventually, they were removed. The remains of these cruives can still be seen today.

One story connected with these fish traps was when a local was seen by the river superintendent taking fish from the cruive and placing them in a large sack. Instead of shouting at the poacher, the superintendent shot him dead! In those days this was deemed to be justifiable homicide for no action whatsoever was taken against the murderer. He couldn't have been a Jacobite!

Another hilarious story from the same era occurred before bridges to the islands had been built. The magistrates of Inverness used to entertain visiting dignitaries, including the Lords of the Justiciary on circuit, in the islands. The only suitable access for these high-ranking personages was, of course, by boat. The entertainment included al-fresco dining on salmon taken alive from the cruives and cooked on a spit.

This went on for a number of years but was stopped when one year, while the party was in full swing, someone released the boats and they drifted downstream. There was only one way back to shore and that was for the magistrates and their guests to be carried over the river. They enlisted the help of some sure-footed locals, overlooking the fact that one of them was a local poacher, Archie Fraser, who proceeded to carry the judge across the river. Archie asked His Lordship why he had been so hard in his sentence the previous day on the poor soul who had broken the nets at Beauly. The judge apparently replied that "all poachers must go under". It was then that Archie mysteriously slipped and dropped him in the river!

There is a pool on the river, on the Bught Park side of the Ness Islands, known as the General's Well which flows past a well of the same name. The pool and well are believed to have been named after a General MacIntyre who resided in Bught House during the 19th Century. The pool immediately upstream from the General's Well is known as the MacIntyre Pool and no doubt owes its name to the same gentleman. But it will be of interest to know that this pool was once known as Rossie Lodge after a large dwelling of that name standing on the east bank. Rossie Lodge is long gone now but has been replaced by two modern blocks of flats which retain the name of the original building on the site.

I do not know the origins of all the pool names on the association water but, starting at the top, the Red Braes Pool is so named as the trees on its banks, particularly on the Caledonian Canal side, turn a most beautiful colour of red in the autumn.

Moving downstream, the Weir Pool name is self explanatory, being below a weir specifically built to funnel water into a lade to drive the generator for the first public hydro-electric scheme

'Look what Daddy caught!' – Paul with a 28 pound fish from the MacIntyre Pool

to serve the town of Inverness. The attractive, stone-built generation house is now the ice cream parlour and shop for the Whin Island children's play park. Just below the weir, and leading down to the Mill Stream, are the Trenches. These were named after the trenches dug by a mechanical digger several years ago when repair work was being carried out on the weir. I personally have yet to take a fish there but several fish are taken from this pool each year. The Mill Stream is so named as it runs behind Pringle's Woollen Mill buildings.

Below the MacIntyre, on the east side of the island opposite the General's Well, is the Provan's Pool, apparently named after a one-time nearby resident. Below the bridge at the General's Well is the Cross Hedges. This goes over a weir into what is known as The Pass which joins the top of the Little Isle, one of the most popular Ness pools.

Continuing straight down from the weir at the bottom of the Cross Hedges, on the Bught side of the small inaccessible island, is a little pot known as the Holey. Grilse are often taken from this pot in low summer water. It also runs into the neck of the Little Isle, which runs down to the Infirmary Bridge. In low water, a gravel island appears above the bridge and is known as the Gull's Feet as gulls always rest there. When the gulls get their feet wet there the river is reckoned to be in perfect ply.

Below the Infirmary Bridge is a magnificent long pool known, on the east side, as the Silver Wells and, on the west side, the Leaven Trees. Continuing down the west side there is, hard against the bank, a fast stream known as the Black Stream. For some reason this little pool is seldom fished nowadays, but that was where I caught my first ever salmon on the fly. The river continues down to the main bridge where, upstream on the west bank, is the Palace Pool after the nearby hotel of that name and the Castle Pool on the east side right below Inverness Castle.

Below the main bridge down to the Greig Street footbridge the waters are known as the Legion Pool, being adjacent to the premises of the British Legion. Below the footbridge is the Friar's Shott. Many years ago, there was a friary in that area and no doubt the friars would have 'shot' a net in this pool. I and my contemporaries remember Logan from North Kessock actually netting salmon there, a practice which we are all glad to see is all but consigned to history.

31

Casting skills cross the generations

On the angling club waters of the River Ness almost all the salmon fly anglers using double handed fly rods use the Spey Cast. The more proficient of these anglers cast lines as long as 40 yards.

As its name implies, the origins of the cast are from the River Spey. I only recently learned, having read Jock Scott's book Fine and Far Off for the first time, that we have to thank the late Alexander Grant for bringing this cast, or a very close variation of it which he called the Grant Switch, to the Ness. My thanks to the late author of Fine and Far Off, Donald Ferris Rudd, for his information about Grant which I am sure he wouldn't have minded me passing on to modern anglers and readers.

Grant, who lived in Carrbridge, practised this type of cast on the River Spey and the Spey cast has evolved as probably the most successful cast for broad rivers. A woodcutter by trade, Grant had a close affinity with wood all his life. Without question he played a large part not only in our local angling history but in most of our double handed fly rod casting techniques.

He was then employed by Lord Burton, great grandfather of the present Lord Burton, and worked in the Upper Garry region of the Ness system. In September of 1889 he landed a salmon weighing 55 pounds on the fly from the River Garry. I wonder if a cast was ever made of that fish?

Grant then moved to Inverness where I believe he stayed at Tomnahurich Farm, now part of the Dalneigh housing scheme, and opened a barber's shop in Baron Taylor's Street. In the small workshop at the rear of the shop he worked at his twin passions, making fiddles and fishing rods. His approach to producing fishing rods was completely different to the then accepted methods. His material was greenheart wood, a close gained tropical wood primarily used in the construction of harbour jetties. He used home-made tools to shape and taper the wood and then acoustically tuned the rod parts with a tuning fork to eliminate dead spots in the length of the rod. Ferrule joints were obvious dead spots and he avoided these by using spliced joints which allowed the rod action to travel unimpaired along the whole length of the rod.

I understand that the idea to use spliced joints came to Grant when he was cutting a customer's hair and noted how the hair lay close together when cut. He even dispensed with cork handles as this additional weight could affect the rod's action. He called his new rods Grant Vibration Rods and took out a patent on them. In the early 1890s he travelled to London to show off his new rods. While giving a casting demonstration on the River Thames he cast an astonishing 56 yards.

Grant apparently believed in single tapered silk lines and I understand he had these made specially for him by a Harris tweed weaver. During the manufacture of these lines the machine had to be adjusted no fewer than 86 times in order to complete the single taper over its whole length. I don't know for certain but guess that these lines would have to have been longer than 50 yards. The lines were square in cross section and they cut through the air with less resistance than a round sectioned line, improving the length of the cast.

I was privileged to have actually seen a Grant Vibration rod in action when, in the mid 1950s, I watched a contemporary of Grant, the late John Redpath who ran Watson's fishing tackle shop in Inglis Street, Inverness. John, who would then have been in his late 70s, was fishing on the bank of the Leaven Trees Pool just downstream of the Infirmary Bridge on the Ness. He was a frail old man who would probably not have weighed much more than eight stone. He was wearing canvas chest waders and brogues and told me that his Grant rod was 17 feet long. The line would certainly have been single tapered silk.

John threw the line effortlessly and as straight as a die across the pool – I reckon in excess of 30 yards. I'll never forget what he told me when I commented on how nice a line he was throwing, "It's the rod that's doing the work, laddie." Oh to have had a camcorder then to capture the ease with which this tiny man handled that huge and heavy fly rod. Incidentally, I remember being told that old John, in his last season's fishing shortly after I saw him, landed 70 salmon from the Laggan Pool of the Ness.

Grant subsequently sold the patent of the Grant Vibration to an Aberdeen company which produced similar greenheart rods under the trade name Playfair. I was lucky enough to have owned a 14 foot Playfair rod with which I fished the Ness and Conon with great success for a number of years. The leather thongs I used to splice the joints together kept loosening, but insulating tape soon sorted that.

In 1895 a local businessman organised a Speycasting competition for local anglers at, I believe, the General's Well Pool on the Ness. Measuring boards were fixed in the river bed and the anglers cast from a boat anchored at the top of the pool. Grant took part in this event and was apparently the hot favourite.

A fellow competitor cast a wonderful 56 yards to equal Grant's Thames cast of a few years previously. Then it was Grant's turn. He cast a phenomenal 65 yards, a new world record. When he set this record in 1895 Grant was using a 21 foot greenheart rod, which certainly weighed more than 30 ounces, and a brass reel of probably five inches in diameter filled with silk line and backing.

The whole outfit must have weighed around 60 ounces yet Grant was able to lift and cast 65 yards of tapered silk line without shooting any line. It really beggars belief!

Having read Jock Scott's description of Grant's Switch cast, I can see only one difference between it and the Spey cast as I know it. Grant allowed only the fly to touch the water above him before he completed his cast with the forward thrust. When I cast – and everyone else I have watched – the line, albeit briefly, touches the water upstream of the angler before the final part of the cast. It beats me how Grant could lift and cast 65 yards of line and only allow the fly to tweak the water's surface behind him before being cast out again, including changing the direction from where the line had been lifted to where he directed it. I just cannot visualise that amount of line being kept up in the air during the cast. It must have been a wonderful sight to see.

I doubt if many modern casters could beat his distance using Grant's outfit so his 1895 record probably could have stood for ever. No wonder he was called The Wizard of the Ness. Photographs of Grant, probably taken around 1900, show him not to have been a big physical man. As John Redpath told me, "It's the rod that's doing the work, laddie." I wonder?

One of the main advantages of the Spey cast over others is that you can cast without the line going too far behind and catching on trees or bushes. One of the greatest exponents of this cast, who I saw regularly on the river for nearly 30 years, was the late Inverness Angling Club president Charlie 'Scout' MacKenzie. Ordinary 30 yard lines were no good to him: he spliced two together! The rod Charlie used for the last few years of his life was a standard three-piece 14 foot glass fibre rod to which he had added an 18 inch butt extension.

Charlie fished the MacIntyre Pool most days and was known there as The Resident. He used to throw a massive length of line.

When I was fishing on the other side of the pool from him his fly would often land within a few inches of where I was wading. He used to catch a great many fish but you could never find out what fly he was using: he always changed it before wading ashore!

Charlie died in 1978. He was found lying with his rod beside him on the banks of the River Conon's Junction Pool. One piece of advice Charlie gave me – although surprisingly he did not practise it – was, "Always cast square, laddie." It was after I began to take this advice that my catches improved and I have since passed on Charlie's tip to many anglers.

My own attempts at casting a fly began after my arrival in Inverness when my rod was a nine foot cane fly rod. The method employed, and the only one I knew then, was a basic overhead cast. I certainly didn't throw a long line.

I then moved on to my first double handed rod, my 12 foot tank aerial, and began attempting to emulate the casting of the expert senior club members. So began my introduction to Speycasting! I lived on the west side of the river then and all my fishing, either spinning of fly, was done from the left bank of the river because of the convenience of access to the pools.

After leaving school and beginning work in Grahams, I found that there were many parts of broken fishing rods about. Using these I fashioned my first greenheart salmon fly rod. It would have been about 12 to 13 feet long, with ferrule joints and as stiff as a poker. The only fly lines available then were silk lines, tapered and level, with the best make being Kingfisher. I could not afford one of these, of course, but there were many old reels in the shop with useable silk lines on them and they did the job for me.

After completing my National Service and returning home, I pretty well picked up where I had left off and got back to the fishing again. It was about then that I acquired my Playfair rod and my first pair of chest waders and brogues. I was then able to wade out and cover most of the pools with the fly rod. My casting improved with practise and on a good day with a slight downstream breeze I could manage to cast 25 and sometimes even 30 yards. This, of course, was all on the left bank off the right shoulder. The right bank was a no-go area as, when I tried to Spey cast there off my left shoulder, I got myself into a right pickle. So I stuck to the left bank because it was so much easier.

Some years after I got my Playfair, glass fibre rods came on the market. I bought a set of blanks for a 14 footer from Bill Brown at Grahams – John Hogg having retired by this time – and I soon made up my first glass fibre rod.

I was now a member of the Inverness Burgh Police. A few days after I had made the rod and the varnish had dried, I went up to the Laggan Pool with Sergeant Armstrong (father of Willie Armstrong, present owner of Graham's) hoping to hook a kelt and christen my new rod. It was around April. We took the boat out and anchored it about half way down the pool. My companion spun while I fly fished out of the back of the boat. I was overhead casting and remember the fly – a Garry Dog single, about size one.

I was very surprised but pleased when I hooked what I was certain was a kelt and handed my rod to Willie, asking him to put a heavy strain on the fish so I could check the bend on the rod and see whether the rod rings were properly spaced. I was well satisfied with the look of the rod's bend and I was even more pleased when we found that the fish was a clean run nine pounder.

I recall that it was later in the same season, while I was practising casting from the right bank of the MacIntyre Pool, that I met George Cameron Jnr. Incidentally, this was the first and only time I ever saw George fishing that side of the river. On seeing my new rod he asked if he could have a cast with it and I handed it to him.

Would you believe, within a couple of casts he was into a fish and I gaffed a nine pounder for him. It was a lucky rod and was my companion in the glory days – fishing Dochfour, Ness Side and the club waters of the Ness, and the Rivers Beauly, Conon, Findhorn and Glass between the early 1960s and late 1970s when salmon were extremely plentiful compared with the present day.

In the late 1950s I married and moved over to the other side of the town to live. It made more sense to fish that side of the river as access was much easier and I began to fish the MacIntyre, my all-time favourite pool, from the Rossie Lodge side. Overhead casting was completely out of the question there because of the overhanging trees. But no matter how hard I tried I could not master Speycasting off the left shoulder with my left hand uppermost on the rod handle. If I waded out far enough from the bank to clear my back cast I could cast out off the right shoulder, place the line at about 30 degrees from the bank and then, by repeating the cast, square the line so that the fly landed where I wanted, almost square to the bank.

There were, however, a couple of drawbacks to this type of cast. First, I couldn't attempt it unless I was well out from the bank and, second, I was having to cast twice. Half the water covered with the second cast had already been disturbed by the line landing there and again when the line was pulled off it. Any fish lying in that area would have been spooked by all this disturbance on the surface. One thing I don't like to see is anglers who are obviously dissatisfied with their first cast immediately picking up the line to have another try, and sometimes even a third. I'll bet they catch few fish on that last cast. I remember another piece of advice given by one of the old anglers on the river, "If you make a bad cast, just leave it and the current will sort it out." How true that is. I've caught many a fish on a bad cast left to the river to correct.

There is another well-known cast which is often used by anglers who cannot Spey cast with the right hand uppermost on the left bank, and the left arm uppermost on the right bank. This is what is called the Half Spey. It is of great value to use in a strong downstream wind when, if the line is drawn upstream of the angler before the final push to complete the cast, the wind can catch the line and push it down on to the angler who is liable to end up with the hook in his sleeve or worse.

The Half Spey entails drawing the line up briskly with the right hand uppermost until it is opposite the angler's upstream shoulder. The rod is then brought back downstream and twisted behind the downstream shoulder where, after a brief pause, it is pushed forward to compete the cast. The beauty of this cast is that the fly is kept well clear of the angler's face and lessens the likelihood of injury. It is not the best for long casts but it is surely better to be safe than sorry! In such conditions, always wear sunglasses, ideally with protective sides. You only have two eyes and they are in grave danger from a fly whipping in front of your face. A hood will also help prevent injury.

I persevered for a few years with a combination of double casts and Half Speys and had a little success with them, although I could not achieve the distance I would have liked. Then I saw a visiting angler fishing my side of the pool using a type of cast I had not seen before. It was, to all intents and purposes, a Spey cast but he held the rod with his right hand uppermost and lifted and pulled the line up across his body until it was in an upstream position. The rod was then pulled behind his left shoulder and he completed the cast with a forceful forward push. I cannot now remember the angler's name but I recall he was a Vet, so I called it the Vet's cast. I persevered with this new cast until I became quite proficient at it, and it was certainly my favourite cast. What I particularly liked about it was that my right and strongest arm was in charge. On a good day I could cast as far as most of my fellow anglers, and who could wish for more?

A relatively new event originating from annual game fairs is Speycasting distance competitions. These now attract competitors from many countries world wide. Alexander Grant's record was the target for all the competitors but his record 65 yard cast stood until 2005 when Ness ghillie Scott MacKenzie broke it with a cast of 68 yards at an international competition held at Belvoir Castle in Leicestershire.

When Scott broke Grant's record he was using a modern carbon fibre rod and special weight forward line on a light-weight reel which together would have weighed less than Grant's greenheart rod. A very big part of his final length of line cast was obtained by shooting line – allowing line held at the rod butt to be drawn out while the remaining line is aerialised during the final part of the cast. Scott won this competition on three consecutive years, 2003 to 2005, and in 2006 the event was won by his neighbour at Ness Castle, ghillie Gordon Armstrong.

Scott MacKenzie   *Gordon Armstrong*

Scott MacKenzie making a champion's cast at Ness Side on the River Ness

Competitive Speycasting is entirely at the mercy of the elements with wind speed and direction being critical. Should the wind happen to change towards the competitor just as he has cast, and as the end of his line is straightening, the line can fall back. Conversely, should the wind happen to pick up in the direction of the cast it can carry the line, adding many yards to the distance and perhaps win the event.

Scott and other British and international casters travelled to San Francisco in 2005 to take part in 'Spey-o-Rama', a four disciplined event organised by the Golden Gate Casting and Angling Club. The event included disciplines which involved casting off both shoulders. Scott won it with the best average score and added another trophy to his collection.

In September of 2006 Scott took part in the Emerald World Masters Competition held at Carlton House, County Kildare, where he captained the Scottish team which included Ian Gordon and Bill Drury from Speyside, Eoin Fairgrieve from Kelso and Gary Scott from Glasgow. The Scottish team won the event and Scott's individual cast of 66 yards was the best in the competition.

The following day, the top six best scoring individuals from the participating teams took part in a cast-off for the top spot. While practising for this event Scott cast a phenomenal 72 yards which, unfortunately, was not part of the competition. In the actual competition Scott's neighbour Gordon Armstrong of Ness Castle – who had qualified as a member of the British team – won with a cast of 63 yards. Systal Knut of Norway was second with 61 yards and Scott took third place with 60 yards.

Naturally, Scott took great pride in being the world champion and record holder. But he did not expect his record to stand the test of time like Grant's. Better training techniques and improvements to rods and lines make it inevitable that his record will be broken. There are already many casters who have the ability to cast even further. I hoped that when the record was eventually broken it might still be held by an Inverness-based angler such as Scott, Gordon Armstrong or Murray Richardson, another Inverness lad whose casting ability resulted in him being picked for the GB team in Ireland in 2006. And so it proved. When competing in the Tweed Angling Fair at Kelso early in May, 2007, Gordon Armstrong cast a phenomenal 73 yards to add the world record to his world championship. But Scott remained competitive, making a cast of 71½ yards.

The fishing tackle company Diawa have, with Scott's collaboration, brought out a new range of 'Signature' salmon fly rods of 12 to 16 feet in length. Courtesy of Diawa, Scott has already visited Canada and is due to visit Japan later in 2007 to demonstrate his skill with the rod.

My connection with the MacKenzie family goes back even further than Scottie. When I came to Inverness in 1947 my family lived in Ballifeary Road, close to Bught Park and a sports stadium where they played an odd game I had never heard of, never mind seen, before. It was not at all like hockey and I learned they called it shinty. Played with a stick called a caman, this game is certainly not for the faint-hearted. It is a fast and furious as the teams charge up and down the pitch, swinging their camans from ground level to as high as they can to reach and hit the ball. While the game involves considerable skill, requiring fast reflexes and the ability to hit left or right-handed with equal accuracy, it inevitably results in players' camans connecting with various parts of their opponents' bodies. Just to watch this game was, for me, too painful. Skull caps were unheard of and shin pads were for cissies. I tried it once or twice but skinned shins were sufficient deterrent to any long-term commitment to the game.

Three doors further up Ballifeary Road lived Scottie's parents, the

MacKenzie family, and I often watched Scottie's father Bill — together with Tommy Cumming and Bill Kennedy, who I still remember from those days — participating in this Highland sport. To me and all the other boys of my age in the street, Bill became a bit of a hero for having the guts to take part in this tough sport. He was, of course, considerably older than me and Scottie hadn't even been born then. Bill managed a motor spares shop and after buying my first old banger I became a regular customer of his, buying spark plugs and other bits and pieces. So my friendship with the MacKenzie family continued, later including Scottie who became a regular visitor to my workshop as I made minnows.

Moving on to the early 1980s, my youngest son Paul — then aged about 10 — was very keen on golf. I have no doubt that, had he persisted with it, he would have become very proficient at the game. But that was before motor bikes — say no more! I was very friendly with Andrew Smart, then manager of the Caledonian Hotel in Inverness, and I was aware that the hotel was organising a pro-am golf competition at Inverness Golf Club at Culcabock. Among the golfing dignitaries would be Brian Barnes and among the celebrities would be Douglas Bader, the World War II fighter pilot ace. Andrew told me that he had arranged for Paul to be Brian Barnes' caddy for the event. I had previously ghillied for Brian on the Spey and Ness and knew him quite well but, thinking of Paul's diminutive physique at that time, said he would have to have a caddy car as he could not possibly lift a professional golfer's bag. This was duly arranged and on the day Paul proudly lined up with Brian and two local golfers as they stood outside the club house waiting to tee off.

Followed by a large and knowledgeable gallery, excluding me of course, Brian parred the first three holes on the course. On the next hole, after striking a magnificent tee shot, he paced the distance between his ball and the green before returning to his caddy to ask for the iron he proposed to use for his approach shot to the green. Along with the assembled gallery, I was dumbfounded when the diminutive caddy – standing no more than waist height to Barnes – turned from the caddy car and produced an iron which he proposed to the golfer saying, "Six iron Mr Barnes?" Although not a golfer, even I appreciated that this just wasn't done in the best of golf circles and the gallery, by their combined gasp, obviously agreed. Brian, somewhat shaken by these events, stammered, "No, no, just give me a five iron please caddy." You can just imagine the crowd's reaction when Barnes' subsequent iron shot bounced clear out the back of the green and a shot was dropped!

But this didn't affect the big fella's game. Teeing off on the 18th he only had to par the hole to break the course record. Turning to Paul, Brian said, "Give me the bazooka caddy" and Paul unsheathed and handed him the number one wood. Following a mighty drive and pacing the remaining yardage to the flag, Brian asked Paul, "What do you think caddy – a number nine iron?" Paul replied, "I think so Mr Barnes" and handed him the iron. It was used with impeccable accuracy to deposit the ball only a few inches from the hole and a tap in gave Barnes the new course record for the Culcabock Golf Course.

Paul received a generous tip for his services and for a long time after that he had a poly bag pinned to the wall above his bed with a note saying, "This is the ball that Brian Barnes used to break the course record at Culcabock Golf Course. Caddy Paul Cathcart."

In the evening of the event I attended a dinner held in the Caledonian Hotel Ballroom and was very surprised to see my old friend Bill MacKenzie sitting at the top table alongside Douglas Bader. I was curious to discover the connection between the two and was very surprised to learn what I am certain very few people in Inverness knew – Bill had been Bader's batman when they had both been incarcerated in Colditz during the Second World War.

32

Fly lines

I have previously mentioned the fly lines I used and my early progression from brown cord to second hand silk lines. These silk lines floated when dry but sank when wet. When greased line fishing – using a floating line – they had to be dried out regularly by hanging them over bushes in a breeze and applying a flotant such as Mucilin – a messy job! This task had to be carried out at least twice during a day's fishing, or the line run on to a line winder at night.

But things were changing. I cannot remember the exact date but it would have been about 1970 when plastic coated fly lines like Aircel and Cortland came on the market. These were available in both floating and sinking versions. The early floaters were dark brown in colour and we found, by trial and error, that the AFTM (American Fishing Tackle Makers) ratings nine or 10 suited most of our 14 foot rods.

The arrival of these new lines completely changed our fishing. No more drying lines or slimy fingers – it was great! I'm sure they helped us catch more fish, especially in low water conditions. I liked a line which sank a little in heavy water and preferred to fish a floater with a short length of ungreased silk line spliced to the end – like a modern sink tip line.

A few years after I began using the Aircel floater, in a brown finish, I saw that they were now being produced in white, so I bought one and put it on my fly reel. You should have heard the comments on the river bank when I began using it. "For God's sake, Cathcart, you'll frighten all the fish in the river!" "You'll never catch fish using that!" "Is that string you're using?"

I was the first angler to use a white line on the Inverness Angling Club waters, but I wasn't alone for long! As I was catching a lot more fish than many others it only took a few weeks for almost everyone to start using them.

The correspondence columns of the angling magazines were filled, for many months, with letters for and against the white lines. Now, all these years later, it has been well proved that the 'fors' were right. White lines are less visible to fish and improve catches. I wonder now just what the old boys would make of the lines I see being used today? – orange and fluorescent yellow, green and even pink.

In the past 50 years we have come an awful long way with regard to almost every aspect of fishing tackle. I wonder, assuming that fish are still there to catch 50 years on from now, what our tackle will be like – rods fitted with sat-navs and fish-seeking lures, or maybe resurrected Playfair spliced greenheart rods and silk lines!

33

Inverness Angling Club

The beautiful broad and clear waters of the River Ness as it runs through the City of Inverness are part of Inverness Angling Club's stretch of the river where members and visitors can enjoy a cast. But it was not always so. Right up until the early 1900s these waters were privately owned and only a privileged few could fish them.

The first recorded meeting of Inverness Angling Club was held on the 31st of August 1917 when it was reported that over one hundred names had been submitted as prospective members. And at a meeting on the 21st of September that same year, the secretary, William Watson – unquestionably the owner of the

Long term angling club members 'Bonto' Jamieson (left) and Bert Kraut at the Little Isle Pool

fishing tackle shop in Inglis Street, Inverness, later owned by John Redpath – was instructed to have membership tickets printed.

There is no doubt at all that members of the club did fish the Ness at the time but records for this period are somewhat lacking as to the circumstances they fished under or which pools. At a meeting on 4th July 1922 John Redpath moved that the club approach Inverness Town Council with a view to the council securing the Bught Fishings, and failing this that the club take action to endeavour to raise the money to purchase them. After lengthy negotiations with the owner of the Bught Estate, Colonel Warrand, its sale to Inverness Town Council was formally sealed on 30th April 1923.

For the 1924 season adult membership tickets were set at £1 1s, juveniles at 10/6d and 5s for under 16s. Visitors' weekly tickets were set at 10/6d until July 15 and £1 15s for the remainder of the season.

In 1926 it was reported that there were problems at the weir where the fish pass had not been made deep enough, and in 1929 the club successfully negotiated the right to fish the Friar and Cherry Shotts – the pools below the Greig Street footbridge and the present Friars Bridge. In the early 1930s the club began an annual contribution of £20 to keep salmon nets off the river mouth and estuary.

Everything seemed to be going fine for the club but in 1951 everyone was shocked to learn that the Town Council had again let out the netting rights on the river at Friars Shott. The average reported catch made by the nets over the following four years exceeded 1,400 salmon and grilse. These catches unquestionably affected the rod catches on the whole river. The club's returns for 1955 of 28 salmon and seven grilse amply reinforced that.

In September 1955, however, the club agreed to offer an annual rent of £500 for the Bught Fishings for seven years, on the condition that the netting would cease. This was accepted and the netting at the Friars Shott ceased for all time. Club catches certainly improved after this with returns of 335 salmon and 39 grilse in 1956, 425 salmon and 33 grilse in 1957 and 392 salmon and 57 grilse in 1958. Club membership at this time averaged around 400, including a healthy number of juniors.

In 1957 the first ever restocking of the club waters was carried out when 32,000 Norwegian sea trout fry were placed in the river. Two years later, 32,000 salmon fry – I believe from the River Oykel – were placed in the MacIntyre Pool.

In those days little was known about the genetics of salmon. It is now realised that little good would have come from these well-intentioned acts as these stocks of fry had not originated in the

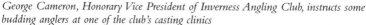

George Cameron, Honorary Vice President of Inverness Angling Club, instructs some budding anglers at one of the club's casting clinics

Ness System. Indeed the genetic make-up of Ness stocks would have been weakened as these alien fish returned as adults and interbred with native salmon.

In 1960 the club staged its first class in fly tying, tackle making and rod repairing at Inverness High School with club president Charlie MacKenzie introducing these skills to anglers young and old. In the same year the last netting station on the Ness – the Stell Fishings situated below the harbour – was bought from Inverness Harbour Trustees by the Town Council and the club agreed to make a contribution of £1,000 toward the purchase.

At the club's annual general meeting in 1962, president Charlie MacKenzie commented that the excellent returns for the season – 470 salmon and grilse – was due in no small way to the increased use of the fly, a very good thing to see.

The use of the fly, and Speycasting, increased steadily in subsequent years to the extent that it was generally accepted that newcomers could not call themselves Ness fishers until they could Speycast at least 30 yards. Responding to demand from members who wanted to improve their casting techniques, the club introduced Casting Clinics in 1974 when – every Wednesday evening in June – young and old would gather at the Little Isle Pool and receive instruction from expert club casters.

The clinics continued for many years with instruction being given by expert casters such as president Charlie MacKenzie, club secretary Jack Fraser, George Cameron, Bob Falconer, Graham Mackenzie and Mike Campbell. The clinics benefited many youngsters new to the game and many late starters to the art, and are in no small way responsible for maintaining the reputation of Inverness anglers for their Speycasting ability. The results can be seen most summer evenings when the expertise of these young fly casters is regularly commented on by visitors and fellow anglers alike – one of our many tourist attractions, I'm sure.

Among other tourist attractions which can be enjoyed during a walk along the riverbank are, apart from witnessing the landing of a salmon, sightings of our resident herons and one or more of the ospreys which nest every year not far from the banks of the Ness. If you are lucky, you will see this majestic bird actually diving into the river and taking a trout. Personally, I don't grudge them these few fish but I have a very different view of the mergansers and goosanders whose numbers on the Ness have increased dramatically over the last few years. I regularly saw different flights of up to 20 fishing the waters of the Mill Stream Pool and then flying off upstream to the Red Braes Pool or downstream to the MacIntyre Pool and beyond.

I understand that these birds can eat up to their own bodyweight of fry every day or so. When you consider that the weight of their individual catch is less than an ounce you begin to realise just how many fish they eat! This is where twitchers and anglers will never agree, I'm afraid. I'm all for culling these birds to a reasonable number which would at least give our all too meagre stock of fry and parr some chance of survival.

Since its birth Inverness Angling Club has benefited from the foresight and strong leadership of key individuals. From the 1920s to the 1940s they included Sir Henry Munro, Dr Kerr, J G Ellis, William Watson, John Redpath, John Fraser, A D Robertson and Warden MacIntyre. In more recent years that strength has come from Charlie MacKenzie, Simon Cameron, Jack Fraser, George Cameron, Bob Falconer, Aeneas Mackay, Graham MacKenzie, Gordon Smith, Don MacKay, Neil Fraser, Mike Campbell and others too many to name. Without them, Inverness Angling Club would not now be so healthy. With people of such stature in the world of angling, Inverness

Angling Club has become one of the finest associations of its kind in the land.

I have had the pleasure of being a member of this fine club for 60 years now and during this time served on the committee and was vice president for seven years. In 2006 I was very humbled to learn that I had been made an Honorary Member. A great honour indeed! I hope to be able to enjoy many more days out on the river and the 'craic' with my fellow anglers.

Inverness Angling Club president Charles MacKenzie gives casting instruction at one of the early Highland Field Sports Fairs at Moy

34

And finally...

When they were children, my two sons Grigor and Paul – and later my three grandchildren Jennifer, Sarah and Darren – were all taken fishing many times and, I'm glad to say, they all hooked, played and landed several salmon each. Unfortunately – or perhaps wisely – none of them became as badly afflicted by the fishing bug as I have been all my life, but I have many happy memories of witnessing their introduction to the Noble Art.

One day I will never forget was in the mid-1990s when the grandchildren were aged seven to ten. It was a lovely September day and I took them to one of our regular haunts on the Coignafearn beat of the River Findhorn. I was fly fishing in a shallow run in front of Frank the keeper's house and the three children and Ilé II were running down the hillside behind the house. Ilé was no more than a black dot running ahead of the children. I stopped fishing and filmed them with my camcorder for a moment as they ran off the hill and across the field towards me. I started fishing again and soon hooked a lively little grilse.

When the children and Ilé arrived shortly afterwards, I gave the rod to Jennifer and she played it until Darren, following my instructions, netted it as I filmed the action. I removed the hook, a size four Red Prawn (my other favourite fly), and returned the fish to the water. Ilé watched it closely until it swam out of sight. There followed an experience which beat even some of my best Canadian days. Within a few casts of recommencing fishing I hooked another three grilse which the other two grandchildren and I each played and landed while being filmed by Jennifer or me. All were returned, much to Ilé's disappointment I'm sure. The sport we enjoyed that afternoon was a once in a lifetime experience. I'm sure that long after I'm gone my grandchildren will tell that story and, perhaps, view the film of our four-in-a-row catch.

In my lifetime I have, through meeting some lovely people, enjoyed some of the finest salmon fishing and deerstalking on wonderful beats and hills. This was particularly the case with salmon fishing at a time when salmon numbers were at their best in the past 50 years. I hope I have managed to acquit myself with a modest degree of success in that field – or should I say river!

My everlasting and favourite memory of salmon angling is wading waist deep in a bold broad stream, bracing myself against the current at my back, handlining in a few yards of line then lifting my fly rod up and behind me and pushing forward to complete the Spey cast. As the line rolls out smoothly I release the few yards of retrieved line and watch with a little pride as, just after the line straightens, the fly – fully extended at the end of the cast – plops gently into the water. It may only be a cast of about 25 yards but a well executed Spey cast is a thing of beauty and a joy to behold. It gives the angler quite a thrill just to have completed it.

I hold the line against the rod butt, underneath my two middle fingers and over my forefinger and little finger, and wait as the cast slowly fishes round towards my side of the river, with the sensitive rod tip feeling the different currents the fly fishes through. Then it happens! There is a long slow pull at the end of the line. I hold onto the line quite tightly and, slowly but firmly, lift the rod against the pull. I feel the unmistakeable shake of the salmon's head as it decides whether to run or just lie there, bemused as to why this attractive object which tempted him to give it a bite should suddenly wish to pull him in.

Without doubt this is the most exhilarating and intimate moment in salmon fly fishing, and the reason we fish. It sets the adrenalin coursing through our veins. Indeed, I know of anglers who are more than content to hand the rod to someone else to play the fish: the take is all the sport they want.

I hope that in future years successive generations of anglers will be able to experience that thrill as salmon numbers return to something like those I had the luck to encounter, and that screeching reels and yells of "I'm on!" once again become commonplace on our river banks.

I have had many pangs of conscience about killing the first salmon I caught at Loch Mhuillidh and the many coloured back-end salmon I killed over all my years fishing in different Highland rivers. But in those days no-one talked about conservation and there were so many fish about then that I doubt if the salmon I killed would have made any difference to the spawning stocks.

Today, however, it is a completely different story and we have to consider very carefully the advice of experts who say that some rivers are not recruiting sufficient fish to sustain a future population. Some believe that the only way to correct this situation is to seek legally enforceable powers to force anglers to employ catch and release. I believe, however, that people best respond to voluntary action, generated by good communications and a positive approach to co-operation. Hopefully, the powers that be will see the light!